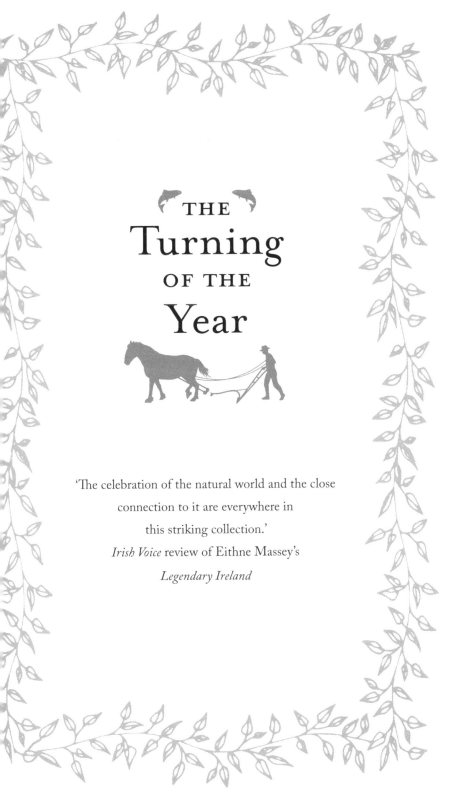

THE
Turning
OF THE
Year

'The celebration of the natural world and the close
connection to it are everywhere in
this striking collection.'
Irish Voice review of Eithne Massey's
Legendary Ireland

First published 2021 by The O'Brien Press Ltd,
12 Terenure Road East, Rathgar, Dublin 6, D06 HD27, Ireland.
Tel: +353 1 4923333; Fax: +353 1 4922777
E-mail: books@obrien.ie
Website: www.obrien.ie
The O'Brien Press is a member of Publishing Ireland.

ISBN: 978-1-78849-211-9

Printed and bound in Poland by Białostockie Zakłady Graficzne S.A.
The paper in this book is produced using pulp from managed forests.

Published in

DUBLIN
UNESCO
City of Literature

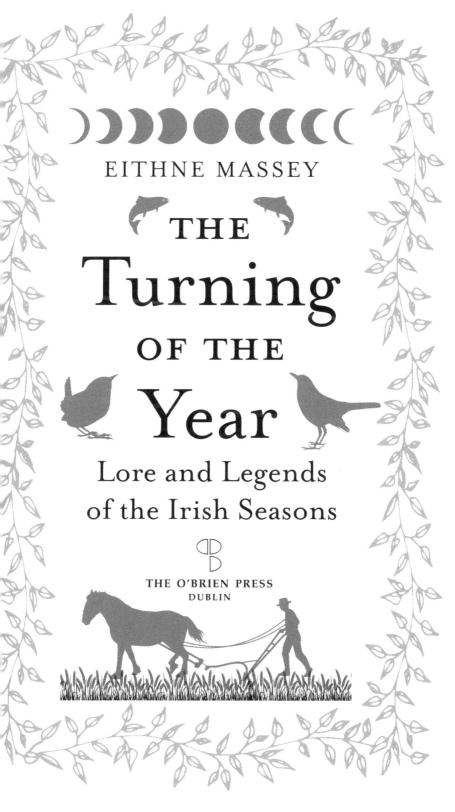

EITHNE MASSEY

THE
Turning
OF THE
Year

Lore and Legends
of the Irish Seasons

THE O'BRIEN PRESS
DUBLIN

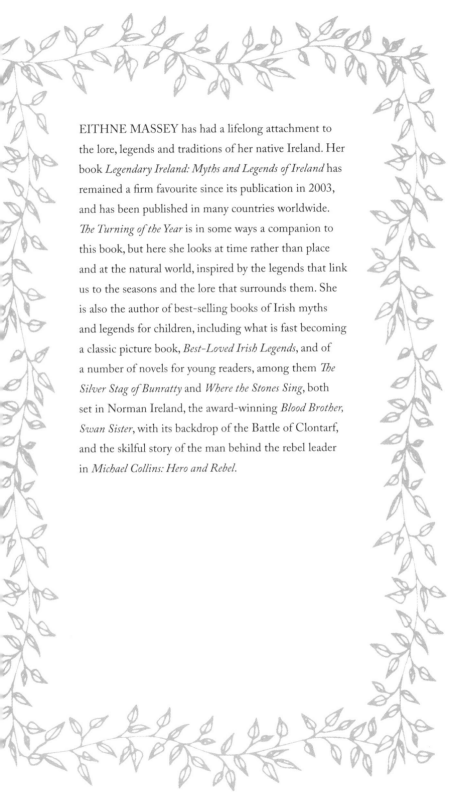

EITHNE MASSEY has had a lifelong attachment to the lore, legends and traditions of her native Ireland. Her book *Legendary Ireland: Myths and Legends of Ireland* has remained a firm favourite since its publication in 2003, and has been published in many countries worldwide. *The Turning of the Year* is in some ways a companion to this book, but here she looks at time rather than place and at the natural world, inspired by the legends that link us to the seasons and the lore that surrounds them. She is also the author of best-selling books of Irish myths and legends for children, including what is fast becoming a classic picture book, *Best-Loved Irish Legends*, and of a number of novels for young readers, among them *The Silver Stag of Bunratty* and *Where the Stones Sing*, both set in Norman Ireland, the award-winning *Blood Brother, Swan Sister*, with its backdrop of the Battle of Clontarf, and the skilful story of the man behind the rebel leader in *Michael Collins: Hero and Rebel*.

DEDICATION

For Julie Howley, 1956–2020:
friend to many and keeper of the seasons

ACKNOWLEDGEMENTS AND THANKS

There were a number of seminal sources for the material in this book. In terms of printed material, the works of Kevin Danaher and Dáithí Ó hÓgáin deserve special mention. Thanks are also due to Eugene Costello for sharing his thoughts on booley houses and their music. To the library workers, both in the National Library and the Public Libraries, a special thank-you for helping me with sometimes long lists of requests. The staff at the Traditional Music Archive were also very helpful. I would also like to express my thanks to those people who helped me with copyrighted material:

Tara Doyle of Dublin City Libraries, Tom Gillmor of the Mary Evans Picture Library, Ailbe van der Heide of The National Folklore Collection, UCD, Jonathan Williams of The Jonathan Williams Literary Agency and Alan Brenik of Carcanet Press.

Given that much of this book was researched in 2020, the ability to freely access the JSTOR collection of periodical articles proved invaluable. It could not have been written without that access, nor indeed without access to the invaluable National Folklore Collection. The material held there, collected from the schoolchildren of almost a hundred years ago, is truly a national treasure. I would like to thank the Director of the Collection, Críostóir Mac Cárthaigh for permission to quote from the Collection (a full list of the quotations used appear in the text credits at the end of the book).

In addition, I would also like to thank all at the O'Brien Press for their hard work in putting this book together, especially Susan Houlden and Emma Byrne. Finally, I would like to thank family and friends for their encouragement and helpful suggestions, which ranged from discussions on the uses of red flannel to information on ancient mousetraps. Fidelma Massey, Tara Huellou-Meyler and Jacques Le Goff, thank you for allowing me to use your pictures and photographs. Jacques Le Goff, who had to listen to me through many a rant when things were not going well, deserves a very special thank-you for his support.

THE DAGDA'S HARP

In Ireland, the year begins in music. The Dagda, the great god of the ancient Celts, had a harp that was a living creature. We are told that when the Dagda played it, the year came forth from the music. Like a tune circling into itself, the seasons, marked by the changing weather and the changing face of the landscape, whirled along in a rhythmic progression. First the gold and red of dying leaves, then the dun of barren fields, then onwards to the whiteness of snowy hillsides and to the green of spring and summer forests. Forward to the gold of the harvest and then back again, to the deeper gold of autumn. The music the harp played was what the hero Fionn called the sweetest music in the world: the music of what happens. What is the music of what happens? Wolves howling, blackbirds singing, the small bleat of a newborn lamb sheltering on a February hillside or a girl calling her cows in from the pasture? It is all of this and more. It is the music that is played in time, as the seasons turn.

CONTENTS

Introduction

THE YEAR IN IRELAND

The dying leaves of Samhain heralded the New Year in the Ireland of our ancestors, in celebrations beginning on the eve of the first of November. The Celts celebrated sacred days from twilight on the day before the festival, and similarly, the year began in the quiet of winter, where life can root and grow, waking to spring on the first of February, Imbolg. Summer was welcomed on the first of May, Lá Bealtaine, and autumn and harvest at Lughnasa, at the beginning of August. Samhain, Imbolg, Bealtaine and Lughnasa – each of our seasons arrives several weeks earlier than is the norm in the rest of the world, for worldwide, the seasons are based on the movement of the sun, on its solstices and equinoxes in December, March, June and September.

In Ireland the division of the year is more closely based on agricultural activity, on the life cycles of the beasts that graze the land and the crops that grow on it. This division is seen in the earliest myths, such as in the story of the Second Battle of Moytura, which was fought between the Tuatha Dé Danaan and the Fomorians. The Fomorians had enslaved gods such as the Dé Danaan god Dagda, forcing him to dig ditches. When the Tuatha Dé Danaan defeated the Fomorians and captured their leader Bres, in return for his life he tells them the secrets of crop growing:

> Spring for ploughing and sowing and the beginning of summer for maturing the strength of the grain, and the beginning of autumn for the full ripeness of the grain, and the reaping it. Winter for consuming it.

In this book, each section will include legends based on the lore, festivals or activities associated with the season. Like each place, each season in Ireland also has a story.

Each of the seasons has a different energy, and different tasks, pastimes, animals and plants associated with it. Each one has a different way of being, a different relationship with the earth. We mark these differences in every aspect of our lives, from the clothes we wear to the food we eat, in our celebrations and holidays and in the dark times when we trudge through each day, hoping that we are heading in the direction of the light. Seasons are also closely related to human cycles of growth, as singer/songwriter Yoko Ono put it succinctly in her album *Season of Glass* – spring with innocence, summer with exuberance, autumn with reverence and winter with perseverance.

The Cycles of Nature and Their Rituals

In the past in Ireland, each turning point in the year was marked by a celebration which, over hundreds if not thousands of years, had become entrenched in the folk traditions of its people. The arrival of each season was marked by distinct customs and rituals.

It is these traditions that we will be looking at in this book. These folk rituals are more than just quaint observances and beliefs. For hundreds of years they brought the community together and acted as a form of social control. They also reflect the special relationship that both the individual and the community held with the natural world. Paying attention to the turning of the year and the natural cycles of the Earth can still be a way of experiencing a direct and powerful relationship with the world of nature.

In the past, this acknowledgement of the natural cycles was seen both in everyday activities and the celebration of great communal events. Today much of this connection has been lost. The balance in the world population has tipped so that the majority of people now live in urban environments. Technology, which has made our lives safer, more comfortable and more interesting, has also blotted out the moon and stars and covered over the green world of natural growth. In recent years horrific forest fires have blotted out the sun. In many parts of the earth, our time and our activities are no longer controlled by the cycles of weather or the cycle of day and night. People live on global time now, most of us in societies where everyone runs very fast, in order, like Alice when she went through the Looking Glass, to stay in the same place. The enforced pause of 2020 brought home to many that their 'normal' way of life was in some ways a toxic one. Some of us learned to call our time our own, though some found their 'free' time invaded by extra work. Either way, our relationship with time changed. Some of us realised that we need time to pause and reflect on where we are and where we want to go. Connecting with the natural world and marking the year's turnings is one way to do this.

Finding Time

Time as a concept has its own history; it is not absolute. Much of the eastern world does not celebrate the New Year on 1 January. Pope Gregory summarily removed ten days from the month of October in 1582 in order to correct the 'drift' that use of the Julian calendar had caused over the centuries; by 1582 the equinoxes and solstices were out of sync with their original dates. The spring equinox was happening ten days before 25 March. This calendar was not adopted in Britain until 1751, nearly two hundred years later and in Turkey in 1927, so even within a quite small geographical area there were periods when not just the daily time but the dates of the month differed between countries.

Humans are also obsessed with managing time by dividing it into periods. At one end of the scale we have aeons, at the other nanoseconds. Few of us can comprehend either.

Most of us do realise that time moves at a different pace according to our environment, what we are doing and how we are feeling. The ancient image of time as a wheel is an international one, from the Great Wheel of the Hopi to the Zodiac of the Greeks. The Greeks also saw time as the great river Ouranus that encircled the earth and, while moving forward, created an unbroken circle. There have been changes in how we see time during the last thousand years, particularly where societies have moved from away from an agricultural base. Time is now seen as something linear, moving towards a future point. Most of us have lived for many centuries in cultures where time is part of the capitalist world view – time is a physical entity: like money, it can be lost, spent, wasted, saved. The Dagda's harp on the back of our Irish coins tells us in a very literal way that time *is* money.

However, we are not so far away from the world of our ancestors as we might think. Many of that world's rituals have been preserved, while others have been transformed into contemporary celebrations. It is estimated that Irish children born in 2021 will have a life expectancy of a hundred and five, a lifespan of over a century. Looking back, we are less than a century away from a time when most Irish people lived close to the land and the changing seasons and their rituals were very much part of our lives. Glancing through the 1911 census of Ireland, you will see many families listed as workers of the land: agricultural labourers, farm domestics, farmers, farmers' sons, daughters. These people worked within the rhythm of the seasons and were dependent on the will of the weather gods as to whether they could work at all. Seasons were their time, and weather and time are deeply linked, even in the Irish language. The word for weather – *aimsir* – is the same word that is often used for time and also for grammatical tenses, how we talk about our past, present and future.

We cannot return to a world of pre-technology. We cannot un-know what we know and no one wants to go back to a world where brutal diseases killed so many and a large percentage of people lived in poverty. Nor do we want to return to the sheer back-breaking toil of subsistence farming; digging rocky fields by hand, hauling seaweed to fertilise the land, piling stone upon stone at the boundaries and bending, lifting, shifting the sheaves of corn to pile them up on a cart for the harvest home. There was a reason thousands of people fled the land of Ireland, not just during the nineteenth century but well into the twentieth.

Lucky Days and Ancient Calendars

If the Sun and Moon should doubt,
They'd immediately go out

William Blake, from 'Auguries of Innocence'

If our grandparents and great-grandparents milked cows and ploughed the fields, herded sheep and dug potatoes, they also tied red thread to the tails of their cows on Lá Bealtaine and left the doors open at Imbolg, guarding against the malice of the Otherworld or inviting its protection into their homes. Even within the weekly cycle, they watched for lucky and unlucky days – days when one might bury a dead animal, start a journey, sell a cow. Depending on the locality, the lucky and unlucky days could vary and even contradict one another, but among the hundreds of entries in the National Folklore Collection it seems that Mondays and Fridays tended to be unlucky days, Tuesdays and Thursdays more fortunate. For some reason, Thursday was an especially auspicious day for curing ringworm. If we look back to when The Triads of Ireland were written, in the ninth century, we find that the three 'woman-days' were Monday, Tuesday and Wednesday; if the woman goes to a man on those days, the man will love them better than they will love the man, and the woman will outlive her partner. This tradition of good and bad days goes back millennia.

The Coligny Calendar shows how the Celts marked time, but its main function was recording lucky and unlucky days. The Calendar is marked on a bronze tablet, which was found at the end of the nineteenth century near Lyon and is thought to date from the second century CE. By this time the Celtic tribes had been heavily influenced by Roman culture – the Calendar uses Roman numerals. The calendar includes both sun and moon reckonings, with the months divided into light and dark sections. Its lunar cycle of nineteen years underscores the importance of the moon's phases to our ancestors. The carvings at Knowth, one of the Boyne Valley sites in Meath, also clearly depict the cycles of both moon and sun. Indeed, the four divisions of the year can be seen as reflecting the monthly phases of the moon – beginning at Samhain at its darkest phase and moving to waxing crescent, full and waning crescent moon.

The Coligny calendar supports the Roman writer Pliny's statement that the Celts of Gaul used a calendar based on the moon, so it is very possible that for them the actual date that each season commenced corresponded with a phase of the moon, most probably the first phase. Therefore, the three days of the Samhain feast would begin on the evening the new moon first appeared in the sky. The 'wild' Irish, we are told by the Elizabethan William Camden, in his survey of Ireland and Britain, knelt in front of the new moon and prayed, asking it to:

Leave us as whole and sound as thou hath found us.

And the moon, of course, rules the tides, the other great marker of time.

The interior of Newgrange.

The Coligny Calendar reflects a society with a sophisticated relationship with the cycles of sun and moon, and this relationship is also seen in the Nebra Sky Disc, a bronze disc that shows the sun, the full and the crescent moon and some stars, including the Pleiades or Seven Sisters group. The disc is much older than the Coligny Calendar. Found in Germany, it dates from the Bronze Age and it shows us that long before the Celts the study and depiction of the heavenly bodies was well established.

The Megalithic Landscape

Our ancestors' knowledge of the movements of the heavenly bodies is seen on a massive scale in the construction of the great stone monuments found all over Europe. In Ireland, the alignment of Neolithic structures to the sunrises and sunsets of the solstices and equinoxes occurs throughout the country, from Carrowmore and Carrowkeel in Sligo to the Drombeg Stone Circle in Cork. But it is nowhere more evident than in the great concentration of tombs in the Boyne Valley. Newgrange, Knowth, Dowth and further west the Loughcrew cairns; so many of these structures are aligned to the sun, the force that made the grass and the crops grow. The mysteries of these constructions are still in the process of being explored and recent advances in genetic science have revealed the scale of the culture that created these passage tombs. DNA studies have found that despite the fact that this type of tomb is distributed over an area of hundreds of kilometres and was built over a period of five hundred years, there are close genetic links between the people buried in them.

The lunar and solar references in these tombs can be seen not just in the way they are aligned in the landscape but also in the treasury of sculptural art that they hold – the most concentrated accumulation of megalithic art in the world, with constantly recurring symbols of spiral and solar wheel. Knowth especially, with its sunbursts, spirals, cupmarks, moons and suns, constitutes a whole bible of symbolism, a lost narrative waiting to be read. Carved on what is known as Knowth's calendar stone, Kerbstone 52, is an image of the phases of the moon over a nineteen-year cycle – just like the Coligny Calendar. Some observers have also linked the alignments and imagery of the site with other astronomical features, such as the Milky Way, Venus and the Pleiades, or Seven Sisters, which appear in the sky from October until the end of April, directly corresponding to the period from Samhain to Bealtaine.

This knowledge of the movements of the stars and the natural cycles is reflected in many of the ancient Irish legends.

The Kerbstone, Knowth.

It was seen as being part of the acquisition of wisdom. King Cormac, the wise king of Irish legend, says:

I was a listener in woods

I was a gazer at stars

We do not know, however, exactly what form this knowledge took. It was not the scientific knowledge we have today. But it seems that these ancient peoples answered some of their questions about the nature of the cosmos, not just in the great stone monuments, but also through story and ritual.

Who calls the kine from Tethra's house, and sees them

dance in the bright heavens?

Who can tell the ages of the moon?

Amergin

Writers such as John Carey and John Waddell have shown the ways in which the myths and legends of Ireland, written down many centuries after the events they recount, can hold within them a hidden code that links them to the lost knowledge of the great stone monuments of Ireland's earliest peoples.

One such theme is the expansion of space within space, a theme which has been carried into modern folklore, for the fairy mounds are always bigger inside than outside. In the stories relating to Newgrange and the Boyne Valley monuments, they also often involve the expansion – or contraction – of time within time. Newgrange acts in some ways as a giant timepiece, a way to understand and celebrate the cycles of time, most specifically that of the solar year. In one Newgrange story, the Dagda makes a day last a year, so that he can enjoy his lover Boann and she can give birth to their son, Aonghus, while her husband is out hunting.

In Dowth, where the tomb's alignment is towards the setting sun at the winter solstice, a story told is that of the sister of the king who built it, Dubad. Dubad stops the sun in its course so that the monument can be finished. Dubad, in this story, is linked to her brother in an incestuous relationship and both are punished for their transgression. There is recent evidence that some of the bodies buried in Newgrange were the result of incestuous relationships, leading to theories of close family ties among a royal elite, similar to those in ancient Egypt. The story of Dubad reflects this and may be part of the web of images that link the stories, the sites, the rituals and the imagery, and even the lost cosmological knowledge possessed by these people. Is the silver chain that appears in so many of the stories, worn by gods such as Lugh and Aonghus, connected to the Milky Way, which author and astronomer Anthony Murphy has identified in some of the Knowth carvings? Are the Morrigan's cattle, linked together by a chain of white bronze, also connected to the Fair Cow's path (another name used for the Milky Way), the path which may well be that of the cow-goddess Boann, guardian of the Boyne River Valley and the tombs it holds?

We do not know why certain stories continue to live, to be told, and others do not. Perhaps the stories that are told and retold are the ones which hold the most important connections, connections which form a web of meaning that can only be grasped intuitively. Stretching the threads or pulling the knots of reason too tight on the connections can sometimes break the thread. We may have to live with half-glimpses, for so much of what we once knew is lost. But even where the story is lost, in many cases the traditions and rituals remain.

Ritual and Tradition

We know that ritual and tradition place order on our world, giving it patterns that reassure us and keep chaos at bay. When we participate in a ritual or indeed a tradition, we feel a sense of security in being part of an activity that stretches back a very long time. If we tie a red thread to the cow's tail, it will be kept safe from the forces we are afraid of and do not know how to control. But in such rituals there is celebration as well as fear; it is not just about protecting livestock. Like a story or an image, or the light of the stars themselves, ritual outlasts that which it represents. The peasants who would not turn a wheel on various days in the year – Bealtaine, St Martin's Day – were not aware that they were acknowledging the powers of the solar god Manannán. They did it because they had been taught that this was the right thing to do. That particular custom eventually died out, as the world became a safer place, a place that was more under human control. Other rituals remain, transformed in some cases, or enacted only by children, but still present deep within us, connecting us directly to the first person to light a bonfire against the darkness of the coming winter and to all the other individuals and groups who have done so since. It was one of us who on a dark

February day lit a rush light to celebrate the coming of spring, tied a bunch of white blossom over the doorway on May Day, hid the last sheaf in the thatch after harvest. One of us was also the person who first told the tale of the girl who looked in a well and became a river, of the boy who found knowledge by sucking his thumb. We may have changed the way our stories are told, but at the deepest level they are connected with the stories, rituals and impulses of those who lived millennia before us, connecting us with the natural world. Throughout this book, I have tried to show these links, the web of meaning woven by traditions, customs and stories, as the year moves on in its constant circling.

The rituals and customs described in this book honour the

natural world, the world that has been our nurse since the birth of our existence. Our celebration of the seasons at once bears witness to our common humanity and moves us beyond it to a connection with the wider universe of time and space and place. Honouring what each season brings, the blackbird's song, the wind against our faces, the opening of a single leaf, makes each second eternal. The earth travels around the sun at more than 100,000 kilometres every hour, yet we cannot feel it moving. There is stillness at the heart of the movement. The world turns and hums, like a hive of bees or a spinning top: and while, as the writer Mary Webb put it, we cannot know why it turns, we and all creatures are part of its 'giddy steadfastness'.

SAMHAIN

Let us welcome the new year, full of things that have never been.

Rainer Maria Rilke

THE YEAR BEGINS

The year begins with a death. The light is dying. The sun in the sky is weaker, paler, its daily route through the heavens low and fleeting. Darkness has the upper hand.

Summer's work is done and sleep is needed, even by the trees, which do not grow between October and February. Most seeds germinate better in the darkness, and the Celts recognised the need for the quiet time; their great days of celebration began in the gestating night, not at dawn; and so their year begins in the fertile, sleeping darkness, not in the light.

Samhain is the name of the feast when the Celts celebrated their New Year. During this time the dead can cross over into the living world, and many of the living enter the realm of the dead. This is the season when mortality rises – the cold and hungry winter of our forefathers. What has been harvested has to be made to last until summer comes around again. This is a time to endure, a time to stay inside, out of the weather. There are no more raids or battles. The battle now is for survival, against the forces of nature and the forces of the Otherworld. Autumn storms batter at the trees and the hedges, sweeping away the last leaves and bringing great sheets of rain on the wind. The earth has been scraped and is ready for the next ploughing, the next sowing.

THE MONSTER'S STORY: FIONN COMES TO TARA

I have played with this story, as the twist in the end is not in the original. But it has always struck me how bored the monster must have become with the continual destruction of Tara. For Fionn, of course, it is a very different story; he is young and this is the first of his great adventures. This is when he proves himself before the High King. This is the moment when he becomes a hero.

~

Men and Monsters.

Or rather, young men and monsters.

Here's one coming down the road now, looking like a rugby player, if they had rugby players in this particular neck of the woods at this particular time. He is tall and broad, and he wants to be a hero. I was like that once, a long time ago. But that's another story.

A hero is exactly what is required at this moment in time. By me and the bag of tricks beside me. Sitting at the gate of Tara in the late autumn sunlight, looking over the green and the red-berried hawthorn trees, a blackbird keeping watch from the wall, a small red dog asleep beside me. The dog doesn't bark, because all of the dogs have got lazy. What's the point of guarding a palace which will soon be burned down by a fire-breathing monster?

The young man salutes me, smiling. Slightly gormless, with more hair than wit. Great hair though, thick and blonde as summer wheat. He has a thumb on him that bears the evidence of much sucking. What a baby.

'Old man,' he says. 'Greetings. I desire to see the king. Are you the gatekeeper?'

At least he is polite. There have been many aspiring heroes that have tried to kick me out of their path to gain entry to Tara. They soon learned their mistake.

'I am not the gatekeeper, just an old man who likes to see what is coming down the road. But you, lad, what is your name?'

'I am Fionn, and I have come to Tara to become a warrior and serve the High King.'

'Coming and becoming are two different things,' I say.

The boy looks puzzled. He looks up at the ramparts, the half-built walls, the deserted building tools and the stones tossed about everywhere.

'Is there building going on?' he asks.

'They have given up. The festival of Samhain is almost upon us.'

'They have stopped to feast?'

'No, they have stopped because a fire-breathing monster burns Tara down every year at this time.'

That always gets a reaction. But the young man looks interested rather than shocked or frightened.

'But what about the king's champions? Do they not defend the palace?'

'They would,' I say, 'But unfortunately they are all asleep. The monster puts them to sleep by playing on his timpán and no one can stay awake to fight him.'

The young man stares.

'The monster plays a timpán?'

I nod.

'The creature comes out of the underworld at the place known as the Mound of the Hostages. He has the strength of a thousand men. The only thing that can kill him is the Birga, the spear with his own poison on the tip of it.'

'And where can that be found?

'Oddly enough, I have it here in my bag.'

Fionn eyes the bag. The blackbird on the hazel bush sings a warning note but of course he pays no attention.

'It is a mad spear,' I say. 'If I take it from the bag I have to keep it covered in leather in a bucket of water to keep it from killing people all on its own.'

I pause.

'You may take it if you want to use it.'

Fionn hesitates. 'Surely, even if I had the spear I would be put to sleep by the music of the monster, wouldn't I?'

'Not so,' I say. 'If you take the point of the spear and press it against your head, the stench of the poison will keep you awake.'

Fionn looks as if he doubts me, so I take the spear from the bag. The boy jumps away. The bird flies away. The dog howls and runs away. The stench is terrible and the spear leaps in my hand like an angry stag. So I put the point back in the bag and hand it, and the bucket, to Fionn.

'Take it. Now go inside and make your presentation to the king and the court and offer to guard Tara tonight. And remember me when tomorrow dawns.'

I could tell you how Fionn went to the king and asked for

leave to guard the palace against the monster Aillen, and how at first the king was reluctant, for such a handsome lad did not deserve to die. How Fionn persisted until finally the king agreed. How on the morning of Samhain, when the court woke up, expecting to find the charred bones of the boy and the palace in black ruins once again, they were greatly surprised. I could tell you how Fionn stood on the ramparts in the darkness of Samhain eve and waited for the creature to creep from the Mound. How hideous the creature was, with scales of all colours and vicious teeth and rabid claws, breathing fire and ready to tear the young man to pieces. I could tell you how the hideous monster took a timpán from under his cloak and started to play the most wonderful music and how all the court fell asleep. All but Fionn, for he held the point of the spear to his forehead and so managed to keep awake. I could tell you how Fionn challenged the monster and the monster roared back at him. How Fionn pursued Aillen the length of Ire-land, finally killing him with the spear Birga as the creature tried to slide back into the Otherworld. How Fionn cut off Aillen's head brought it back to Tara to present it to the king, when he woke, sleepy eyed but proud in the morning. And how as a result Fionn was given leave to lead the Fianna and became one of Ireland's greatest heroes.

I could tell you one last thing, how Fionn looked for the old man at the gate to thank him, but he could never be found. I could tell you that heroes need monsters, but monsters need heroes too. I could tell you all this but my head has been taken from my body. Samhain is here.

Everything is ready to sleep. And I need my sleep, so that I can dream myself into the future, and wake then to find other heroes, newer monsters.

Hazelnuts.

The Festival of Samhain

Every grove has reddened its berries, the woods bend
to calm weather, on the hazels, the blackthorns and the
brambles; their fruit breaks forth from the dark jutting
bough. Each oak bough has bent, the clusters of nuts
on every hazel, that has not shed its fruit has split with
ripeness, the crop of every apple tree has burst forth ...

Giolla Brighde Mac Con Midhe, thirteenth century

The feast of Samhain was held during the three days between
the end of October and the beginning of November. Samhain
is also the name of the season from November to February and
literally means the end of summer. Before the last fall of leaf
and withering of fern frond, the Celts celebrated wildly; huge
fires were lit, the spirits of the ancestors were honoured and
the forces of the Otherworld were acknowledged and in some
cases invited inside. Tlachtga, the Hill of Ward in County
Meath, was the main site of the Samhain festival. A great fire
was lit and carried from there to the royal seat at Tara, twenty-five kilometres (fifteen and a half miles) away. Feasts were
also held at the other royal sites, such as Rathcroghan in the
west. Monsters were killed and the Otherworld was opened
up; the legendary warrior Fionn defeats the monster Aillen,
and the hero Nera leaves the human world and finds a new
life with the Sídh when he leaves the safety of the court of
Queen Maeve on Samhain Eve.

Before the stillness of deep winter sets in, it was time to set
the hills ablaze with bonfires and shout and sing as loudly as

Tlachtga or the Hill of Ward, County Meath.

possible. And so we continue to do, for Samhain is the Celtic festival that has survived today in the form of our Halloween. Even in its current Americanised, commercialised form, with its plastic pumpkins and skeletons, its basic elements have been preserved.

The aim of Halloween has always been to make us believe that there is something out there in the darkness that is neither human nor necessarily benign. The traditional Gaelic Halloween, which carried the traditions of the Celtic Samhain down through the centuries, contained the same elements of today's 'fright night'; and many of the pranks had exactly the same aim – to make someone jump. Bonfires have transmuted into bangers and fireworks. Children continue the tradition of dressing up and doing the rounds of the neighbourhood, begging for treats.

Nowadays the original three-day feast is concentrated on

Halloween itself (31 October). All Hallows or All Saints' Day (1 November) and All Souls' Day (2 November) mark the traces of the original three-day festival. Both feasts, which celebrate the dead – the blessed and the not so blessed – were established much later than the original festival. The celebration of these feasts at the time of the ancient Celtic festival mingles the Otherworld of the Sídh with the Afterworld of Christianity in a way which makes one type of uncanniness drift and mix into the other. Though it marks the eve of All Saints' day, Halloween has always been closely associated with the souls who did not make sainthood, the wandering ghost, the unquiet grave. In some cases, crosses were woven at Halloween and hung over the door to keep bad luck away, but unlike Lá Bealtaine, which is all about keeping the uncanny out, at Halloween the dead were welcomed in. The doors and windows of the house were kept open so that the dead could access the family home, and food and drink was left out for them. At this time, all over the world, traditions acknowledge the presence of those that have left the world of the living, from the visits to graves on La Toussaint in France to the celebrations of the Day of the Dead in Mexico. For at this time the dead have their rights. The chairs must be set around the fire, the fire left lighted, the door unlatched.

Sometimes the dead come to take the living away with them, and perhaps this is one of the reasons for the emphasis on disguise, on dressing up, during Halloween night. Disguise has always been seen as a protection, as in the case of Aran Islanders dressing their little boys as girls so that they would not be taken by the fairies. (Girls were obviously considered of less interest to the fairy hosts.) In terms of any community, a festival that involves disguise sends a message that the disguised person has become someone other than themselves. In practical terms disguise also makes it harder to identify the tricksters. So the disguised person is granted a level of social immunity, no matter how outrageous their actions. This immunity can add a sense of threat, particularly to those at odds with the community. Halloween could be a time for settling scores, and those considered cranky or anti-social were at greatest risk of being the butt of tricks and scares.

Halloween Night

As a child in the 1960s, I remember that my mother, who hated Halloween, would nevertheless get in supplies and set everything up for the games that were still played at that time. We ducked for apples and hunted the silver coins of the time, stamped with the hare, the horse and the bull in basins of cold

Halloween Night.

water. We played snap-apple, the saucer game and blind man's buff. Our feast was made up of the bounty of the summer, pears and apples and nuts and more nuts, mainly the sacred and most easily available, the hazelnut. Champ or colcannon, boxty and barm bracks were eaten, all of them with symbols buried inside. The food was about divination, not taste. Futures were told – a ring to marry, a pea or a rag for poverty, a thimble for spinsterhood, a coin for wealth. In the nineteenth century, for those of marrying age it was a chance to see who their future spouse might be. Couples roasted nuts together at the fireplace and if the nuts jumped apart in the heat, it was a sign that there would be no lasting match made. Some of the games were more sinister. In the saucer game the player was blindfolded and had to choose between a number of saucers, each of which foretold a different fate. A coin or ring brought wealth or marriage within the year: but a twig meant a violent spouse, a prayer book meant a religious vocation, water meant emigration and clay was the omen of early death. Some of the older traditions recorded in the National Folklore Collection describe complicated methods of divination using fern seed, gathered at night by 'two men with strong nerves'.

Strong nerves were needed to go outside into the dark on Halloween night. There are many stories of those who dared to visit churchyards hearing the voices of the dead, of bells ringing from under the ground, of the Púca carrying foolish travellers away on his back. Halloween was also known as Púca – or in English, Pooka – Night. The noise and ruckus of Halloween is the noise made to frighten away the spirits, but it is also the shout of the solitary traveller on the lonely road, the noise made to give courage, to break the silent darkness. The howls that came out of the darkness were not always human: some came from the Banshee.

The Banshee

The Banshee, whose name literally means the woman of the fairies, keens and sings and combs her long white hair. She is closely connected with the Hag, the Cailleach, the ancient Veiled One who reigns over the dark and cold part of the year. She is the Badbh, (the Bow in places such as Wexford) the skaldcrow, rejoicing in the blood of the battlefield, but also

The Banshee as a cloaked figure.

mourning the loss of dead heroes. The wail of the Banshee was a wordless *ochón*, like the sounds made by professional keeners, some of whom, it was claimed, became Banshees after their death. The ancient Irish clans had their individual Otherworld guardians, such as Cliodhna of Carraig Cliodhna near Macroom in Cork, warning them of a death in the family. Aoibheall, the Banshee of the O'Briens, was heard keening the night before Brian Boru was slain at Clontarf.

But the Banshee also has other forms. She is sometimes the fairy woman who comes to inspire poets and to call on heroes to fight for her. In the seventeenth- and eighteenth-century Irish language vision poem, the Aisling (the poem form is named after these dream-visions), she is Ireland herself. In folklore she can be beautiful, a bare-footed girl with long red hair. Usually, her hair was pure white: she could be seen combing it, just outside the kitchen window, or watching from a ditch at the side of the road. Like mermaids, Banshees are very attached to their combs, and if it is stolen for any reason, they will come looking for it. The trick to get it back to the Banshee without harm to oneself is to hand it to her through the window on a pair of tongs or a shovel, which will come back twisted and broken – as your arm would have been if you had handed the comb directly to the Banshee. This is one account of many accounts of the Banshee from the National Folklore Collection:

About twenty years ago, my father heard a banshee.
A woman named Mary O'Donnell was sick. The banshee was walking on the tops of the bushes. It was in the

Sumer-time and my father was milking the cows outside in the fields. When the cows heard the banshee, they began to run through the fields and they would not let him milk them. So he had to bring them into the byre to milk them. In an hour after, the banshee went over to the house and tapped at the window and the girl died. Then the banshee disappeared.

Sleeping and Waking

Samhain: when summer goes to its rest.

Emer, in 'Tochmarc Emire',
from the Táin Bó Cúailnge, c. eighth century

Despite its frightening nature, Halloween also held an element of reassurance. The hatches are battened down and we are safe in the homestead for the winter, everything enclosed, from the crops to the cattle to the turf from the bog, giving a sense of completion and comfort. But this good fortune came with the responsibility still to be open to succouring the travelling stranger, whether it was a wandering storyteller or *tincéir*, or someone from beyond the grave. Hospitality has always been one of the greatest social responsibilities for the Irish and part of this tradition was the need to provide a fitting send-off to those who died. In traditional wakes of the eighteenth and nineteenth centuries the dead person at a wake was as much a part of the proceedings as any of the living, and could be offered snuff and whiskey by the mourners, or even a hand of cards.

Even today, Irish funerals are exceptionally cheerful affairs; a focus for family, friends and community to come together and share memories of the one who has died. There are no invitations given, and it can be looked on as a sign of disrespect not to attend some part of the funeral rites, no matter how nebulous the connection with the deceased might be. Politicians still make a point of attending local funerals. The wake, held between the death and the funeral, is still very much part of Irish life today. Through the centuries it has performed an important social function; acknowledging the loss the community has sustained through the death of one of its members, while channelling the grief of those who have lost a loved one.

The wake gave its name to the American Wake, the send-off for those emigrating across the Atlantic, for in the nineteenth-century emigration was so final that the son or daughter, sister or brother, beloved or friend, might as well have been going beyond the grave, never to be seen again. Although the 'wake' – that punning word that seems to hold so many meanings – is said to come from a prayer vigil on a saint's day, there are elements of the Irish version that seem to owe more to the funeral games of the pre-Christian Celts. Irish wakes were seen as pagan affairs, encouraging wild outbursts of both grief and licentiousness at a time the community should be celebrating what was hopefully the ascent of the lost one to the ranks of the blessed.

At its most primitive the wake could involve numbers of women screaming – either to keep evil spirits away, or to make sure the spirit of the dead person did not return to haunt the house. Windows were opened to release the spirit, mirrors covered and, in what seems like an attempt to stop time in its tracks, clocks were stopped.

As early as the late seventh century and throughout the Middle Ages, Irish bishops issued fierce prohibitions against wakes, but with little effect. In the late nineteenth century there was an especially strict injunction against wakes, as recorded in a newspaper in Windsor, Berkshire, England on Saturday, 22 December 1877, which also gives a vivid description of a traditional wake:

In the wilds of Connaught, when a peasant dies the whole country side hastens to the wake. No invitations are given, all comers are welcome, the more the merrier. Plates full of small pieces of twist tobacco, about an inch and a half long, and plates of snuff—hence the saying, perhaps, "Flying about like snuff at a wake"—are left near where the corpse is laid out for the guests to help themselves. The latter bring with them such quantities of whiskey as they can afford and the night is spent in drinking, smoking, story-telling, singing, and "coorting." No dancing is permitted, but the cabins are usually so packed with "sympathisers" that to jig would be impossible. The very idea of such scenes being held over departed Christians is sufficient to disgust cultivated minds, but the action of the Irish bishops is not dictated solely by sentimental considerations. Numerous instances have occurred of late where infectious diseases have been spread broadcast through the instrumentality of wakes, and more than one

medical officer in England has called attention to the evil
caused by the observance of the custom by Irish residents
in this country.

Even this lurid account of a wake does not include the wild
and violent wake games that were played and the fact that
there might well have been dancing in the outhouses, where
the young people would gather away from the crush of
mourners in the house. The wake games – or 'amusements'
as Séan Ó Súilleabháin called them – were often very rough
ones, trials of strength and ability, like those held at ancient
funeral games.

After the games and music, the smoking, the praying and
the drinking, the storytelling (Ó Súilleabháin mentions a
storyteller who got most of his tales sitting quietly under the
table in wake houses and listening hard), all taking place against
the background noise of keening, there was a procession to the
church and then the graveyard. The National Folklore Collection records the numerous piseogs, or superstitions, around the
burial itself. The coffin had to be buried facing the rising sun, or
if that was not possible, facing the tabernacle, the most sacred
part of the church, where the host was held on the altar. Falling
while one was in the graveyard was a very bad sign, and one
should never be the last to leave – that should be the caretaker
or 'some old person'. Cups should be left in the graveyard, as the
soul of the latest person to be buried had the task of bringing
water to the other inhabitants. In the Samhain story of Nera's
adventures in the Otherworld, it is the corpse that suffers from
a terrible thirst that Nera must help him assuage.

THE SKALDCROW'S STORY:
NERA IN THE OTHERWORLD

This story survives in an incomplete form and the narrative is disjointed, but compelling. Set at Crúachain, the western court of Queen Maeve and Ailill, this tale may have lost some of the detail of the narrative in its telling, but none of the strange sense of the Otherworld, of shape-shifting, of moving between different realms at the time of Samhain. There is a sense of a forgotten ritual seeping into the action, which makes it not so much a story as a dream half-remembered and somewhat dis-membered. Some of the details echo what we know of the bog burials of the Iron Age — why is it necessary, for example, for someone to pin the hanged man's legs together with a withy, the strong but flexible branch of willow, in order to keep him from shrieking and calling out? Withies were used in the burial of sacrificial bodies, perhaps for no other purpose than to keep them still — but they may also have a ritual significance that we don't know of. And we are given no information on the two hanged men — were they criminals, captives, or even Samhain human sacrifices?

Some of the action in the tale foreshadows as well as echoes. In popular culture Halloween remained a time to predict the future (as in Nera's vision), when the dead speak and the hosts of the Sídh are able to cross into our world and we to theirs. The early emphasis on fire and water reflects the Halloween customs that have survived until today, while the danger result-ing from not emptying out the water used for washing at night comes up again in a much later tale. It is also a story with a very

strange relationship with time; in it, present and future are folded into one another.

I have made some small changes to the narrative in the interests of coherence, and omitted the connection with the beginnings of the Táin, but I recommend a visit to the original to those interested in the darker and wilder reaches of Samhain.

~

Samhain. Ailill and Maeve were in Rath Crúachain, the winds howling outside, the sky darkening early. They had long ago moved on from buttermilk to drinking white and red ale and they were becoming quarrelsome, comparing herds and flocks, boasting of their individual prowess in the bed and on the battlefield.

Outside, the wind howled and clouds scudded across the sky. No moon to be seen tonight. Two dead captives were hanging at their doorway, screaming and shrieking, putting Ailill off his roast pig. Maeve wasn't bothered.

Ailill growled into the darkness, 'A withy tied around their feet would shut that pair up. Whoever can do that, that man will have a prize from me.'

There was silence. Samhain, the night when every evil spirit, every wicked demon and púca and sprite in the land was abroad, was not a night that anyone wished to leave the rath. Great was the darkness of that night, and greater still the fear of what might be abroad in it.

Ailill said again: 'Whoever can tie a withy around the feet of the hanging men will have a prize from me, a golden sword.'

Still there was silence.

A third time, Ailill said: 'Whoever can tie a withy around the feet of the hanging men will have a prize from me, a golden sword.'

Then one of the warriors came forward and said he would go out to the hanged men. He was shaking when he left and was back within minutes, shaking even more. Others followed, but it was too fearful a night for any one of them to approach the gallows where the dead men moaned.

And then Nera, the handsome one, the brave one, said:

'I will go.' He took a bundle of willow wands. He took his scarlet cloak and turned it inside out, for that is one way to keep safe from the Sídh. He drew it close around him and tied it with a silver clasp.

Outside the storm screamed louder than ever, but even so he could still hear the shrieks of the captives. In the faint green light Nera could see the men, whirling in the wind where they hung on a small thorn tree. Every fox and hare and badger was buried deeply in its burrow. Every bird was taking shelter where it could. Except for me, the skaldcrow, who loves the howl of the wind. And who was waiting for the hanged men to stop moving so that I could feast. Huddled in his cloak, Nera struggled through the wind to where the bodies were hanging and grasped the legs of one of them, a young man with black hair. As he grappled with the man's ankles, the captive kicked and wriggled and Nera cursed. Something very odd was happening. No sooner did he have a withy tied than it sprang off. Three times he tried, and three times the same thing happened.

The shrieking stopped. Laughter, almost as fearful as the screaming.

Then a voice said, 'For mercy, put a proper peg in it or it will never hold.'

The black-haired corpse was speaking.

Nera said nothing but he broke off a piece of willow and bored a hole in the withies that bound the man's feet. He pulled the peg through it and it held. And he did the same with the other corpse. The screaming and kicking ceased, and the black-haired corpse said: 'I am thirsty to the death here. Take me on your back and bring me to where there is water.'

So Nera took the man on his back.

They came to a house surrounded by a lake of fire. The

corpse said: 'I will find no water here.'

They came to one surrounded by a lake of water. The hanged man would not enter that house either.

Then they came to a house where the slop pail and bath water had been left inside after dark, as should never be done at any time, much less on Samhain eve. The hanged man drank and spat in the faces of the people of that house, so that they all died.

Then Nera brought the captive back to the gallows, and hung him up there, where he swayed quietly now. When he turned back towards Crúachain he saw that the palace had been burnt to the ground, and the heads of his people were being carried away by the hosts of the Sídh. He followed the Sídh until they came to the fairy mound, the cave of Crúachain, and followed them inside.

I did not go in: the hanged men were still now. I had not finished my meal when I saw him come out, his cloak tight around him as if carrying something in its folds. But I left my dinner and followed him into the rath, where Maeve and Ailill were still feasting and fighting.

There he told the strangest tale:

'I went inside the fairy rath, for I saw Crúachain burnt to the ground and the Sídh carrying the heads of my people into the mound. And inside it was summer; and the place was so beautiful that I never wanted to leave. I fell in love with them all, men and women. I was brought before the king, and the king sent me to serve a woman of the Sídh, and my task was to bring her firewood every day for a year. And the woman was very lovely, and we were happy together.

But one evening she sat me down and said: 'You must go back to your own people.'

'But they are lost and Crúachain is destroyed. I saw it with my own eyes.' I answered.

'When you saw the palace burnt, it was a vision of the future, of what will happen this coming Samhain, not last Samhain when you tied the withy around the dead men's feet. So you must go,' said my wife, 'And tell Ailill and Maeve that they must attack the fairy mound, and carry off the golden crown hidden in the well, and the magic shirt and mantle, or the king of the Sídh will destroy them.'

'But I have been gone so long …'

'When you go back, they will think you have only been outside the rath a short time. The meat will still be cooking in the pot, the fire will still be high.'

'My love, why do you tell me this? For this will bring the destruction of your people.'

'Not the full destruction. Take me and the son that will be born to us, and all our cattle out of the mound, and perhaps we will return here after the slaughter is done.'

So I left the mound and came back here. And here I am. You must invade the rath before next Samhain, before they attack you, and bring out the wonders I saw there, the golden crown in the well, the shirt and the sword.'

'Why should we believe your story?' asked Maeve.

Nera opened his cloak, and inside there were summer flowers and fruits.

'The woman told me to take back to you the fruits of summer, wild garlic and primrose and golden fern, so that you would l know that I have been in the fairy mound, and that I speak the truth.'

And when they saw the flowers of summer, Maeve and Ailill believed him.

So at the end of the year the armies of Maeve and Ailill went to attack the Sídh mound. But Nera went before them and took his wife and child and cattle out of the mound before they attacked. And when the battle was over, Maeve and Ailill had possession of the golden crown and the magic mantle and the shirt. But still Maeve looked at one of the calves that Nera had, and she coveted it.

For his part, Nera looked around them, and it was dark and cold in the realm of humankind. So he and his wife took their child and their cattle and the golden sword and went back into the mound of the Sídh, and they may be there until this day, for all I know.

I did not follow them; once again I was busy with other things. There was great feasting that day. I remember it so well; the softness of flesh, the crunch of small bones, the blood to drink.

Wailing Women:
The Caoineadh and the Cailleach

My love and my beloved!

Your corn-stacks are standing,

Your yellow cows milking.

Your grief upon my heart ...

Eibhlín Dhubh Ní Chonaill, 'Caoineadh Áirt Uí Laoghaire',

eighteenth century

Apart from the licentiousness associated with them, there was another reason for the Church's objection to traditional wakes. The Bean Caointe, the keener at the wake was a powerful figure. She could be seen as competing with the priest at this key moment. There are ecclesiastical complaints about wailing women at deathbeds from as early as the start of the sixth century. However, the Church's objections had little effect. There were a number of activities reserved for women, and attending at childbirth and the death were two of them. When a woman gave birth, the Bean Ghluine was present; the Bean Bháin had responsibility for laying out the corpse and the Bean Caointe led the group of keening women who presided at the wake. These could be local women, and if one became known as a good keener, it could often be an unwelcome interruption to your daily routine – but it would have been unheard of to refuse to attend the deathbed. In other cases the women were professional keeners, paid for their services. The keen relieved the tension of grief by giving it a public expression. In some cases the keening was a wordless cry, or a single word repeated, but it could also take the form of a poem. The word keen comes from *caoineadh* – crying, lamenting – and it was a highly ritualistic activity, a chant and a sob, but one with structures and motifs and patterns, with formulaic phrases used and repeated, woven into personal details about the deceased. It was both a eulogy for the dead person and an expression of primitive grief that goes back to our earliest history. Keening had died out by the first part of the twentieth century – by the 1930s' Folklore Survey even the elderly could not recall it happening at wakes. In one story, Leitrim teacher Seán Ó Céilleachair tells of an incident 'about sixty years ago' where the keeners were 'made a laugh of' at a funeral and they felt so insulted that they refused to come to the next wake. The keening tradition stopped abruptly when it was mocked; the traditional respect for the Bean Caointe had gone.

'Caoineadh Áirt Uí Laoghaire'

But up until the end of the nineteenth century, the keen or *caoineadh* was an art form which in the hands of a master – or rather a mistress – could become something exceptional. The best known and the most powerful example of the Caoineadh is also one of the most accomplished poems of the eighteenth-century Gaelic tradition. 'Caoineadh Áirt Uí Laoghaire' influenced a number of poets in the nineteenth and twentieth centuries and is still influencing poets such as Nuala Ní Dhomhnaill and Doireann Ní Ghríofa today. The *caoineadh* is traditionally held to be a spontaneous outburst of lamentation, but in this poem, as in so many other cases, there is high art involved. It manages to combine a public ritual-istic form with deeply felt grief. What is especially striking is that the poem survived in spoken form, passed on by word of mouth from the eighteenth to the twentieth century, when it was finally written down.

The author is a woman lamenting her husband. Eíbhlín Dubh Ní Chonaill was married to Art, a dashing officer in the Austrian army, who was rather too fond of wearing his silver sword and swanning around on his fine horse for the taste of the local Sheriff of Macroom, Abraham Morris. Eíbhlín Dhubh was one of the large family of O'Connells of Derrynane in County Kerry, a wealthy clan of smugglers who kept the traditions of the old Gaelic households alive, including that of creating poetry that was improvised and performed to mark a major event. Eíbhlín had already com-posed a lament for her first husband, who died soon after their marriage, but the love of her life was Art, whom she spotted riding his mare when visiting her sister in Macroom, County Cork. Against the wishes of her family she married the young soldier and by the time tragedy struck she had two children with Art and was carrying another. The ongoing bad blood between Abraham Morris and Art had come to a head when Art's horse beat Morris's in a race. Morris demanded that Art sell him his horse for five pounds. Under the Penal laws, as a Protestant, Morris had the right to purchase the horse for this low sum. Catholics were not permitted to own a horse worth more than this and if requested by a Protestant to sell, they could not charge more. Art refused to sell his horse and had to go on the run. At the beginning of May 1773, Morris, who had been told that Art had threatened to kill him, had him shot by local militia. Art's horse raced home, and Eíbhlín, seeing the blood-stained beast, leapt onto it and raced to where her husband lay. Her description of the discovery of her husband's body has a savage immediacy. The movement of the poem – which plays with the tenses of the present, the past and the future – is complicated, showing the build-up of Eíbhlín's happy world as Art's wife, mother of children and mistress of a household, and then the stripping away of this world. We are shown a world of plenty, a golden world of red berries, amber nuts, floods of apples, wide hospitality. We see and feel the feather bed where her children were conceived and born, the bed she finds refuge in with her two small boys after the death of Art. We are shown how a death can sometimes take away not just a beloved but a whole world. Eíbhlín vows that she will give all her possessions, all the things that warmed and softened her world, in order to gain hard justice for her husband's death. The last bed we see is that of Art's final resting place – his lonely grave, weighed down by earth and stones. The images of plenty, of prosperity, of Art as the giver of largesse, of potency both in terms of sexual prowess and the fertility of his lands, are in stark contrast to the bleak last line which commemorates his burial in Kilcrea Friary. Throughout the poem the images burn into the reader's mind as something genuinely felt, really seen. This is a real horse, this is a real woman, this is a real feather bed.

But the poem also hints at meanings no longer accessible, meanings that are lost or just glimpsed. Eíbhlín tells us that when she finds her husband's body there was no one with him but 'an old wasted woman, covering him with her cloak'. Later in the poem this figure appears as the 'dark little women of the mill'. The Hag of the Mill is a figure from the ancient Gaelic world, appearing in some of the oldest tales. She is the withered old woman, the veiled and cloaked one. The crone is the woman who Eíbhlín will eventually become, the hag who is also the goddess of war and blood; who vows revenge on Morris and will do anything it takes to get it. The quest for justice has left her cold and hard as winter. Although Eíbhlín never got any kind of justice for Art, her voice creates its own form of retribution, travelling through the centuries to us through all the other voices who have taken up the lament, telling the tale of past loss that in the telling, conquers time.

The Veiled One

This mourning figure, banshee, hag and widow is the Cailleach, who is the patron of Samhain, the time of the year that has no shining saint or golden god to act as its guardian. Her name comes from the Latin *pallium*, or cloaked, and when she spreads her cloak on the ground all growth stops. Halloween snaps its jaws tight on the last of summer and the tree line is stark against the sky, the sun a huge white ball that seems to hold no more light than the moon. The Cailleach strikes the ground with her staff, and the first frosts come. Of Iberian (or Maltese) origin and as Beara, the Spanish Princess, she gave her name to the part of Ireland most associated with her, the Beara Peninsula. 'The Lament of the Hag of Beare' is a poem that mourns lost youth and strength, for the hag is of immense age. She is the protector of herd animals, most especially cows in Ireland and deer in Scotland. But she can also be destructive.

The writer Douglas Hyde tells an especially resonant tale of the caves at Gleann na mBíorach (Valley of the Horned Ones) in Kerry, where the hag was responsible for a terrible bovine plague, and in response the last living bull, a huge black creature, brought death to her, her son and her mother, in the shape of a heron and a dog. Horned hags appear in folktales, while other folk traditions tell of Cailleachs who seem to have been real people, local healers.

One of the attributes of the hag was the ability to leap over great distances; the Hag of the Mill out-jumped the mad king Sweeney, though the Hag in Clare could not out-jump the legendary hero Cú Chulainn. It makes me wonder if the Cailleach legends owe something to female shamans who went into trance-like states and travelled to the world of the spirits, returning with messages to the community. But shaman or deity, she is someone who does not want to be seen clearly, not unlike the beggar women who walked the roads of Ireland, wrapped tight in their cloaks. Welcomed in the lonely farmhouses for their skills in knitting and telling stories, they also gave advice that saved children from sickness and harm when the efforts of doctor and priest had failed.

In Scotland there is some evidence of a priestess cult associated with the Cailleach's worship. She is a very powerful presence there, as old as time, pre-dating even the ocean. She sings, in *Cailleach Bheag an Fhásach*:

What time the great sea
Was a grey mossy wood,
I was a joyous little maiden,
I would lift my skirtful of nuts,
Between the two Tormasies.

All over Scotland there are mountains and lochs bearing her name. She is the embodiment of what the writer Robert Mac-Farlane calls 'deep time', the time it takes for landscapes to form, the ebb and flow of the earth She is also an earth-shaper in Ireland, with tales associated with her found from Meath to Cork. Of immense size, she formed the landscape in places such as Loughcrew in County Meath, one of the richest megalithic sites of Ireland. Flying high over the hills (the Slieve na Calliagh or in Irish, Sliabh na Caillí, the Hag's/Witch's Mountains) at Loughcrew, two hags battled to see who could leap the highest, while carrying an apron full of rocks, rather than nuts. Finally one of the hags flies so high that she comes crashing to earth, and rocks and hag and all become stones, the megalithic structures on the tops of the hills. Thus features such as the Hag's Chair and other monuments which may predate Newgrange were formed. The Equinox Stone in Cairn T is illuminated at dawn at the Spring Equinox. The Cailleach is also associated with 25 March, the time around the spring equinox which is also celebrated as the Feast of the Annunciation. She is sometimes the bitter, biting old woman and she is particularly associated with cutting, freezing winds. Her reign stretches until St Brighid's Day, when spring defeats her.

The Cailleach thus holds sovereignty over the land and the weather which shapes it. She is the reason why humans cannot walk at birth. The Cailleach puts her hand on the baby's back, weakening it, making it a dependent creature for longer than the calf or the foal that struggles to its feet straight after birth. In the tiny figure of the newborn, human weakness, but also its resilience, is honoured.

One of the most constant features of the Cailleach is that we cannot look at her face, for she is always the Veiled One. The year 2020 was one when people in western societies were forced to overcome the unease that the masked face traditionally brings with it. Like those in disguise, faces that are caped, cloaked, hooded, bring a sense of threat – what have they to hide? Why do they not want us to know who they are? The Elizabethan English complained about the native Irish

Woman in the Irish cloak or mantle.

living in their mantles, a distinctive fringed cloak called a *brat* that could be easily drawn over the face. By hiding their faces behind long fringes (*glibeanna*) and the folds of their cloaks the Irish could escape identification.

In the sixteenth century English poet Edmund Spenser said the Irish mantle was 'a fit house for an outlaw, a meet bed for a rebel and an apt cloak for a thief', and he also had some hard words for the women who wore the female version, especially the messengers, the mona-shul, the walking women. The walking woman wore smock and mantle only, he claims, in order to make herself 'more ready for her light services'. In other words, in a woman, wearing the Irish mantle was a sign of loose morals as well as a devious nature.

By the mid-1800s, when Samuel and Anna Maria Hall were writing their accounts of Ireland, women were still wearing their mantles while walking the roads. The Halls considered that the heavy cloak with the hood that could be pulled down to cover the face meant that Irish women took less pride in how they dressed, as the state of their inner garments was hidden. To these English travellers, wearing the Irish mantle was still an encouragement to Irish slovenliness.

The cloaked and veiled figure is at once the Sean Bhean Bhocht of the songs of Irish struggle and the shape-shifting goddess who can take the form of a wild doe, a cow or an elk.

Shuffling, bounding, sharp shanked, blue faced, sometimes with only one eye, the hag can transform into a heron or a rock, and from a crone into a young beauty. In some later Celtic tales, such as those of Niall and Lugaid Laighde, she is sovereignty, the dispenser of the power to rule the land.

As the season moves on, the Cailleach brings with her the year's darkest moments. Between Halloween and Christmas, the days continue to shorten, fall into themselves. The winds come in and shake the last leaves from the trees. St Martin's Day on 11 November was another day for marking time, in this case the blood feast of November. It was the day on which animals were slaughtered for winter meat. There are still some tales in the National Folklore Collection of a goose or some other fowl being killed on this day. St Martin is the patron saint of domestic animals, and the blood of the slaughtered beasts was thrown on the doorways of byre and stable. Amhlaoibh Ó Suilleabhain, the early nineteenth-century diarist, notes that the animals or fowl killed on the day should also be shared with the poor, as St Martin shared his cloak with a beggar. Today St Martin's Day marks the commemoration of other blood spilled, the soldiers who died in the First World War. Was the choice of the date of Armistice Day deliberate? St Martin is also the patron saint of soldiers.

So we move further into the silence of winter. Everything – fields, trees, landscape – lies bare and stripped, until the covering of snow brings even more stillness and sleep to the earth. There is a great beauty in the transforming power of snow and ice, the shapes and hollows of the earth starkly defined against ice blue skies. Farm animals are already carrying the young ones they will give birth to in the spring; the cows were put to bull in early May and ewes were put to ram in September. Some of our native wildlife, such as hedgehogs, bats and frogs, hibernate or put themselves into a torpid state until the earth wakes again. There is some evidence that our Neanderthal precursors may have also practised a form of hibernation through the very coldest parts of the Ice Ages. Sleep – we all do it together, more or less at the same time, and yet it is an intensely personal experience. Sleep allows us space and time to move into the most private of worlds, the world of dreams, where each dream is uniquely ours and yet part of the larger picture, the universal world of archetypes. We are still. We shut our eyes, our mouth, our ears.

> This is my story
> The stag belling
> The winter snow
> The summer gone

Ninth-century Irish poem

Christmas and Midwinter

The old man told him not to take the holly because it was fairy holly. The boy did not listen, and he gathered the holly, and off he went home. About a month after this occurrence, the boy had to be taken to a lunatic asylum. The people said that the fairies punished him for taking the holly.

National Folklore Collection

If nature sleeps, humans, as usual, decide that they must wake it up. With everyone at a low ebb some brightness is needed and Christmas obliges. We have seen how the solstices were of huge significance to the people who built the ancient monuments, such as Newgrange, where at dawn at the winter solstice light flows through the hole above the capstone, reflecting on the carved stone and the bones of the dead piled at the end of the main passage. The midwinter return of the sun reassured the community that light was returning, that growth would start again and life would continue. If the origins of a midwinter feast seem to be closer to the Roman feast of Saturnalia, or, with its trappings of Yule log and evergreens, to Scandinavia and Germany, rather than to Celtic tradition, it seems that a long time before the Celts arrived in Ireland, the people of the country marked the winter solstice in the most permanent of ways, celebrating the rebirth of the sun. In more recent times, Christmas has become the archetypal family feast, and its customs bring light and comfort. The candle in the window, the presents left in stockings hung on the bedrail, the dark green of ivy and the bright red of

the holly berries used to decorate the house: all of them help us through the dark time. Christmas was also a time when the community came together, at fairs such the Big Market, which was held before Christmas. This was where dried fruit and other Christmas luxuries such as the goose or spiced beef were purchased, to be consumed with immense pleasure after the Advent fast. The Market was also a chance to meet those people who lived at a distance and were rarely seen. Christmas Dinner was the major feast of the year and food was a huge part of Christmas, more so than in any other festival. Even the animals were given extra food.

The religious ceremonies were joyful and filled with song. Some areas had special carols, notably Kilmore in Wexford. The dead were not forgotten: on the three days around Christmas, wreaths were (and are still) brought to graveyards and on Christmas Eve, in many houses, food and drink were left out, not for Santa or Rudolph, but for those who had died during the year. There was a tradition that on Christmas Eve, donkeys and cows were granted the power of speech and could be seen kneeling in the stable and byre at midnight. Candles were lit in the windows and a single one left alight all night, to guide the Holy Family. This custom is honoured still, in Áras an Uachtaráin, the home of Ireland's President.

For the children of the 1930s who took part in the Schools Folklore Project at a time when Ireland was poor and rural, it was a bright, high point in the year, the greatest of the celebrations, with feasting and gifts and brightly decorated houses. The food and drink that played such an important part of the festivities were associated with specific traditions. As Peggy

Mc Cullough from Louth put it:

> Long ago the people used to be watching Christmas more
> than now-a-days. They People used only to drink tea on
> Christmas night. Now the people drink tea every night, so
> they dont be watching christmas so much.
>
> This is a custom connected with Christmas. All the
> people make a Christmas pudding. They don't cut it till
> Christmas day. They say it is unlucky to cut the pudding
> before Christmas day. If the pudding breaks when they are
> boiling it they say they would be dead before next Christmas

> National Folklore Collection

The sense of joy and wonder, the excitement of the child, can
still make Christmas something more than the orgy of spending and self-indulgence it can sometimes seem to be.

On St Stephen's Day the much more pagan festival of hunting
the wren took place. The tiny bird with the loud voice is no longer
hunted, killed and nailed to a pole, but in some towns the wren
bush is still carried around the town, decorated with silver balls
and accompanied by musicians and mummers in fancy dress and
straw hats, the colours indicating their local loyalties.

In the Dingle parade, the most well-known enactment, a
hobby horse plays an important role, as does the man dressed
as the old woman, the Cailleach. The wren had a reputation as
a magus, a magic creature, the druid bird. Folk legends give a
rationale for his killing – that the bird called out and alerted
the Danes, or in some versions Oliver Cromwell, to the presence of Irish soldiers, and his descendants must suffer for his

Hunting the wren.

crime for eternity. In other versions the wren is the bird who betrays St Stephen, patron saint of 26 December and in one particularly wild story from Kerry, the wren pinches Fionn Mac Cumhaill's ear to warn him the Orangemen are coming. The wren is said to nest in a holly tree and is killed with a holly stick, then interred in the wren bush, coffined and keened, its funeral games held. The wren is also credited with being the king of the birds, though it achieves its sovereignty by trickery.

> The wran the wran, the King of all birds.
> St Stephen's Day was caught in the furze ...

The other bird closely associated with Christmas is the robin, the doyen of the

Christmas card. The association of this bird with Christmas seems to date from Victorian times, but it is a bird that has always seemed to hold a special place in human affections, probably because of its cheery friendliness. The robin is very much in evidence in December. In late December, he sings, marking his territory and finding song posts from which to proclaim his lordship over a particular patch of ground. The legends associated with the robin connect his red breast with the blood of Christ and also with fire – in every case the robin is trying to help another being, whether it is a god or the two lost children who die in the woods. The robin is a friend of many.

The December festivities continued into the New Year, and New Year's Day had its own piseogs – it was unlucky to throw out ashes, give away milk or spend money on that day. Little Christmas or Epiphany is on 6 January and is the celebration of the adoration of the Magi. In Ireland, it was known as Nollaig na mBan. This is when the women of the house put their feet up after all the hard labour involved in the Christmas celebrations. There can be magic in the air on this date – it was said that water becomes wine, rushes become silk and gravel becomes gold. In recent times it has had a revival as a quasi-feminist, Celtic Christianity festival. After the sixth, the crib and decorations were taken down, with some of the greenery kept to make crosses with on Shrove Tuesday and the holly stored to burn in the fire on which the traditional pancakes were cooked on that day.

The long hangover that is January has arrived. The very dead of winter, when the Cailleach's face is blue with cold. A hawk spirals, watching its prey in what's left of the stubble of a cornfield. Now the air is sharp and the edges of the trees and bushes have a surreal clarity. Snow and heavy frost bring with them a sense of a world made clean and new, a playground for the young but a trap for the unwary. It is only in the muddy days of the snowmelt, when the ruts on the road thaw and freeze again, that we realise that even snow leaves its detritus. January, seemingly the longest month of the year, has the virtue of strength in the face of icy winds and freezing rain. We keep putting one foot in front of the other, with faith that the world is turning towards the light, knowing that journey has started already. We watch for the first sign of spring, the snowdrops in the sheltered corner of a field, the beginnings of leaf buds on hedgerow and tree. We wrap up warm and hide in our houses, out of the cold. From the fire of Halloween to the ice of January, we have traversed the themes of Samhain: mourning, keening, sleeping, waking. And we acknowledge the darkness. The fields are dark, brown soil dense with water or hard as rock with ice, merging into the bog.

THE MESSENGER'S STORY: THE MAGIC MANTLE

This is a late medieval story that appears in different forms in many parts of northern Europe, notably in the stories of King Arthur's court, where the action occurs at the Feast of Pentecost, which falls in late May or early June. It felt more suitable to set it in the depths of winter, when the gatherings of Fionn's followers may have become a little strained. Fionn is associated with the wildness and freedom of the hunt and the forest, but there were long winter days when hunting was not possible. It is impossible to say if the story has any 'Irish' roots or is simply a retelling of the other versions. Whatever the origin, it is still a good story. In one version Conán kills his wife, but I have taken a lighter approach to the ending. I have also made the narrator a Walking Woman, the Messenger, the cold eye from outside the group. These female messengers were the ancestors of the walking women that were still part of Gaelic Irish society in Elizabethan times, and their descendants may well be the female storytellers who walked the roads of Ireland in the twentieth century. The story is set at Almu, on the Hill of Allen, a small hill rising up out of the bogs and plains (and at that time forests) of Kildare. It was the historical residence of the ancient kings, and traditionally Fionn's winter quarters.

~

Hot. Stuffy. Smelly too, to be honest. The smell of humans, hounds, cats, songbirds. All part of the great court of Fionn, where I have been stuck these two weeks. Two weeks is too long to stay stuck anywhere, especially a place full of Fionn's followers and their women. Drinking, boasting, perilously close to fighting. I am sickened by the clash of the silver goblets, the smell of roasting hog and deer, of human sweat. I should have left with Caoilte before the ways became impassable. He invited me to come with him to the forests, to listen to the music the wolves make in winter. But he had more on his mind than listening to wolves and I had my next message to deliver, far to the south, and did not wish to be diverted by either wolves or men. I need air. I will walk out and say hello to the robin in the holly bush by the entrance. He makes more sense than everyone in the court put together.

But here is the gatekeeper, flustered, woken up from a long wine-induced dream, for no one has come to and no one has gone from this place since Caoilte left. The snow has hardly stopped falling and the view from the hilltop is of whiteness: white forest, white plains, white bog. All mantled in snow, pure and hard against the fierce blue sky.

'There is a maiden at the door,' says the gatekeeper. 'She requests admittance to the feast.'

'A maiden,' shouts Fionn. He is flushed and loose-lipped, a wine cup in his hand.

'How did she get here in this weather?'

The doorkeeper shakes his head. 'I just looked up, and there she was. She is alone, and she must have come on foot.'

'Let her come in then,' says Fionn. 'Perhaps she is in need of help. We would not refuse shelter to a dog in this weather, much less a maid.'

The doorkeeper hesitates. 'I think she is no ordinary woman, mighty Fionn.'

'Well, if she is extraordinary, all the better!'

Fionn straightens himself in his chair and pulls in his winter paunch. He has no wife at present and he has always found a wife a good thing to have during the long dark days of Samhain, when hunting is impossible. How he – the greatest of all the hunters in Ireland – misses the hunt: the belling of the hounds, the sight of a doe leaping ahead of him into the unknown!

Everyone sits up and pays attention, eager for diversion. The court is like a witch's brew of intrigues and emotion, all brought to a boil by being stuck inside. The women gossip, scratching at each other with their tongues. As for the men, as hangover runs into hangover and all the boasting that can be done, has been done, tempers are beginning to fray. Conán, the mischief maker, the angry man, sits sprawling and red faced by the fire and demands more drink to toast the arrival. He clashes his silver goblet against that of Fionn and spills the red ale over his cloak.

He calls to his daughter, who is playing chess with her mother, 'Take this away and fetch me my red one.'

Before she turns to her father, the girl raises her eyes to her mother, who nods briefly. Then she makes her way to Conán and takes the cloak from him.

'Isn't she beautiful, so beautiful,' boasts Conán, catching his daughter's arm. 'More beautiful than her mother was at that age. The poets sang songs about my wife, but now their songs are of my daughter!'

The girl's lips tighten and she tries to pull away. Conán's wife is watching him from the other side of the fire. She is still beautiful, but she is no longer young. My eyes meet hers, and she blushes, and suddenly she looks as young as her daughter.

But now silence has fallen. For the doorkeeper has brought the woman in.

It is true that she is no ordinary woman. Tall and straight as a willow wand, with fair hair and green eyes. She wears only a light mantle, which at first seems white but then seems to glow and glitter with all the colours of the room; the flame of the fire, the gleam of the gold and silver goblets, the reds and blues, saffrons and duns of the Fianna mantles. And then, finally it is green, a green that we have not seen since the very first birch leaves unfurled, in a spring that seems a hundred years ago.

She bows to Fionn and her voice is like the sweetest music: 'Hail, great Fionn. Thank you for allowing me to come to your feast.'

'Indeed you are welcome, lady. Will you not take a seat, and some refreshment?'

'A little water mixed with milk is all that I require. I thank you.'

She looks with disfavour at the venison roasting on the spit.

'Now, sweet lady, tell me why it is you come here? Do you need the help of the Fianna?'

The lady smiles.

'It is not help I need, mighty one, but only some company. And I hope I can give some entertainment to your company in exchange.'

At this every man who has not already sat up straighter does so.

Conán says: 'And what form does the entertainment take, my lady? Are you a singer, a musician? A poet, a storyteller?'

The woman smiles again, aiming the full force of her green eyes at Conán.

'Rather, I have a game to be played, a dare to be made.'

'We will never refuse a dare!' says Conán.

'Very well,' says the lady. In one graceful movement she removes her mantle and the court can see that she is even more beautiful than they had thought. Her gown is silver-grey, edged with red gold.

'Come, gather round me.'

She is smiling.

'This cloak,' she says, 'has magical qualities. If a man puts it on, and he has ever told a lie about his deeds, it will shrink, getting smaller and smaller according to the size of the lies he has told. The closer it reaches to the ground, the more honest the wearer is.'

'That is a good game!' This is one of the ladies.

The men say nothing.

'Is there anyone who would wish to be first?'

There is a certain amount of shuffling, shifting from foot to foot. The lady looks at the circle around her, smiling still, but with a glint in her green eyes.

Conal says: 'Fionn, you are our leader and the first amongst us. And we all know of your great deeds, for you have told us of them. You should be the first to try the cloak.'

Fionn gives him a filthy look.

'I will be first of the men then, but surely it is better that ladies should be the first to try this new game. Does it have the same effect on them?'

The lady's smile widens and she says: 'Not quite the same. With the ladies, it shows if they have ever been unfaithful to their husband.'

Again silence. Fionn smiles. He has never been so glad to be wifeless.

'Very well then, ladies. Shall you start the game?'

Oscar's wife steps forward, pushed ever so slightly by her husband: 'I will be first.'

So the lady places the cloak over her shoulders; it covers her to mid-calf, and everyone gasps. Blushing, she removes it.

Then the other ladies come forward. On some it reaches to the knee, on some no further than the elbow.

There is only one woman in the place who is covered to her feet by the cloak — the steward's wife, but she is ill-favoured and bad-tempered, so no one is much surprised.

Then Fionn notices that Conán's wife has been hanging back from the game. It is time to get his revenge.

'Your wife, Conán, surely she is the most faithful of spouses. She should try the cloak.'

Conán's wife pleads with her husband with her eyes. Conán shrugs — his wife has to be faithful, the old hag that she is. Surely there is no risk here.

'Go ahead, woman,' he says. 'Try it. Put it on.'

The woman places the cloak on her shoulders. There is a gasp. Conán's wife covers her face in shame. The cloak is no more than a ruff around her neck and she stands like a statue, her eyes downcast, her cheeks as red as fire.

But then there is a noise from her daughter; she has her hands over her face and I wonder if she is crying. Then I realise that what is coming from her mouth is laughter. It spreads: the whole court erupts into hysterical mirth.

Conán makes for his daughter, but Oisín takes his arm on one side and Oscar on the other and Fionn says quietly: 'Let it be, Conán. No woman shall suffer harm as a result of what has happened today.'

He turns to the stranger.

'But my lady, perhaps your game has gone on long enough?'

'Yes! Let that be the end of this crazy game!' screams Conán, still trying to free himself from the restraining arms. 'And you, woman, get out of here with your accursed cloak! As for whoever has dishonoured me with my wife, I swear I will find out who it is and kill him!'

I say nothing and Conán's wife's eyes meet mine once again.

The stranger woman smiles. She takes her cloak and walks out of the hall.

I am not part of their game. This is not my place, I have merely been stranded here by the snow. I came with a message for Fionn, for that is my task in life, a messenger from one place to the other. Now it is time to move on.

I go outside, to gauge the weather and see what direction the lady has taken. The wind has changed: it is from the southwest. Already, the melt has begun: a patch of red fern on a south-facing hillside, the colour of red rusted iron, dried blood, the pelt of an old fox. A long journey ahead of me, through plains and bogs and bitter winds. I will leave tomorrow, before the sun rises. I will not stay to bid farewell to anyone. I look for the traces of the stranger's foot. But there are no human prints on the snow. Only the delicate prints of a small, running deer.

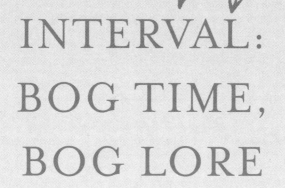

INTERVAL:
BOG TIME,
BOG LORE

A piece of bog deal had to show light to the women that
were spinning.

National Folklore Collection

IRELAND'S BOGLANDS

The darkness of the landscape leads us out beyond the last cottage of Irish towns and villages to that place where bleakness reigns. And there, too, there is much to uncover of Irish lore. Bogger, bog trotter, Bogsider. Bogman – the insult used by the townie for those who lived in the country. The bog is not just a place, but a people. The word comes from the Irish for soft, but the softness of bogs is the softness of treachery and deception; for our wide bogscapes draw the eye and the foot to unsafe places. In a cold and wet country the edge of a bog is one of the coldest and wettest places to live, with no shelter from wind and driving rain. But bogs can also be places of celestial beauty, with sunset skies that challenge the coming darkness in a sweep of gold and red glory. Bogs are as horizontal and desolate as deserts, but like deserts, they are not without life. The landscape of a sunny summer bog, with its white *ceannbhán* (bog cotton) flowers and the soft haze stretching into the distance, smoke rising from small cottages that border it, is that of child's story, with gentle donkeys and wild swans breaking the blue of the sky. Such a landscape brings with it a sense of freedom rather than restriction. There is a further contradiction at the heart of bogland; the bog can be up to ninety-eight per cent water, but what comes from it, dried and stacked, has kept generation after generation warm through the winter. In the past, turf was a hugely important resource in the tree-poor landscape of Ireland. Turf fires give little flame; they smoke and sulk and create a vast amount of ash. They are also the scent of old Ireland, the flame of the home fire.

Each bog is a living, growing system, but one which grows at such a slow pace that it is hard to grasp. The peat gathers and holds memories from the most ancient times. Plants and trees and animals; once all individual lives, now make up a part the landscape, a single entity. Like trees with their rings, the layers of a bog are a physical manifestation of time, of the ages it has lived through, and of the people who lived near it.

The Céide fields, on Ireland's wild Atlantic coast, in the most remote and bleakest part of Mayo, are the site of the oldest known field systems in the world, dating to 5,500 years ago. Originally discovered during turf cutting in the 1930s, the lines of rock hidden beneath the bog mark out pastures and tillage fields from a time when the climate was warmer, and vast pine forests had been cleared for agricultural land. That clearing of the forest cover resulted in the eventual destruction of that community, for the forest canopy had prevented the earth from becoming saturated with water. Water fell and fell and the land became bog, covering the traces of the ancient farmers.

Blanket and Raised Bog

Sometimes a bog shifts, moves or bursts. Blanket bogs, which are located on the sides of mountains and are mainly found in the west, can slide off the side of a mountain. The National Folklore Collection tells us of many bogs that 'ran away'. Blanket bog, the Cailleach whispers, is the coverlet, the mantle that protects, hides and keeps warm.

The other type of bog, the raised bogs that make up a large part of the midland counties, are much deeper than blanket bogs and beyond prehistoric – some say 9,000, some say 7,000 years old. (These figures put the history of the 2,000 years of Christianity into context: the era of AD becoming an ellipsis between possible beginnings). Raised bogs are much deeper than blanket bogs and cover the land to a depth of between seven and twelve metres. Most have their origins in the gradual infill of ancient lakes, the shallow lakes left when the glaciers passed, where vegetation grew and decayed. Peat is made up of the decayed remains of organic matter. One of its main elements, sphagnum moss, creates an environment which acts as a preserving agent to any organic material buried in the bog. For thousands of years, for reasons known and unknown, objects, animals and humans have been added to the witches' brew of our boglands. Perhaps they were buried to preserve and protect, perhaps to destroy or hide. As bogs change over time, so they change what they hold, what humans have lost in them or concealed in their depths.

The Secrets of the Bog

The secrets of our bogs bring us back long before the Celts. We share the heritage of bogland with northern Europe, particularly Denmark. Much work has been done during the last decades to discover the stories bogland has to tell us. As the bog is stripped of its cover, it gives up its secrets. The ancient routes of roads have been mapped, settlements marked, field systems uncovered, artifacts found. Tubs of humble bog butter, buried to keep it fresh, have been found, some dating from the early twentieth century, some from the Iron Age.

It is now widely accepted that many of the objects placed in bogs were not simply lost, but were placed there as ritual objects in ceremonies that we can only guess the purpose of. There are some 3,500 archaeological sites in Irish wetlands, in rivers, in lakes, in fens and bogs. Nearly all of the Irish prehistoric cauldrons that we know of were found in bogs, though none of them as impressive as the huge Gundestrup Cauldron, found in a bog in 1891 in Jutland. Weapons, jewellery, otter-skin cloaks, drinking vessels were all buried. Wood and leather, horse harnesses, model boats, weapons. Some of the weapons are models, some have been ritually damaged so they cannot be used again, and some were crafted as ritual objects, such as the bronze shields that are too delicate for use in battle.

And along with the bridles and shields and great bronze trumpets, we have found human bodies, the most moving and enigmatic sacrifice of them all. The bodies that are found all over Europe, but most commonly in Denmark, show marks of sacrificial killing. The bog acts as a kind of tanning agent on the skin of these bodies, preserving them, because when spaghnum dies it releases polysaccharides that block bacteria from metabolising the body. The flesh is left, tanned by the bog water in what Seamus Heaney describes in *The Grauballe Man* as 'opaque repose'. Tollund man, that picture of repose, had a violent return to the surface from his bed in the bog. One of the Danish helpers had a heart attack during the removal of the body. The bog claimed a life for the Tollund Man's return to the world of the living.

Some of the bog bodies were killed by being hanged by a leather rope, some strangled by a flexible hazel bough. Grauballe man had his throat cut, and the girl found in Jutland's Juthe Fen had crooks holding down her knees and elbows, the branches pinning her into the bog. At Domland Fen in Schleswig the bog girl, whose cape of roe deer skin could still be identified, was drowned in the bog. Sometimes the bodies can be seen to have been strangled and stabbed and broken, as if the ritual involved different ways of ensuring the sacrifice was acceptable. At Borre Fen, also in Denmark, they found peeled white slivers of wood, possibly used in casting lots as to who should be sacrificed.

In Ireland, most of the bog body discoveries are more recent ones, the result of the twentieth-century intensive machine cutting of bogs. Many of the bodies that were found are of young men who had been well treated in the period before their death, and who may therefore have been members of the aristocracy. One of the most convincing theories is that these men were unsuccessful applicants for the kingship of the tribe. Others may just have been outsiders, someone different from the rest of the tribe, or someone who had broken its laws.

Old Croghan Man was found in Offaly; at almost two metres tall (six foot six), he was unusually tall for the period he lived, sometime between 393 and 201 BCE. Back in 1821 the Gallagh man was found in a bog in Galway. His cloak was made of deerskin and the cape was tied at the neck with a band of willow. Cashel, Clonycavan, Stoneyisland: the bog people have become the place names, for we will never know their personal names or their histories, only how they were killed and, sometimes, what their last meal was.

The Bogs Laid Bare

All of these bog bodies were kept safe for hundreds, sometimes thousands of years, wrapped up in sleep in their wet, cold bog blanket. But our bogs are also being stripped bare, like a bed or a sacrificial victim, mainly for fuel but also for garden peat. The exploitation of Irish bogland has become a major environmental issue, for like great forests, boglands are an essential part of the eco-system, helping the earth to breathe, acting like forests to remove CO_2 from the atmosphere and emitting it when cut away. During the twentieth century vast swathes of boglands were cleared for the turf used in electricity production. Now this has stopped, and efforts are being made to rehabilitate and restore some of our ancient boglands, but turf is still used as a fuel for open fires, both in a compressed factory form and in the form of the traditional sod.

Smoke from open fires – including turf fires – adds to the carbon emissions that humans have been producing at an increasingly catastrophic rate. But prohibiting turf cutting by individual bog owners is an emotive subject for people whose families have cut turf for generations. In 2016, 3,000 people still harvested their own turf by hand and went through the laborious process of cutting, stacking, drying and then transporting to the home place. In the nineteenth century cabins of turf were thrown together and lived in, and if things got really tough, the walls could, and sometimes were, burned for heat.

Despite its importance in the home, the bog does not figure as largely as we might expect in the National Folklore Collection stories. Most of the tales are of buried treasure, mysterious lights and murderers hiding bodies in the bog. There are many accounts of gathering rushes for rushlights, of making items such as furniture and candles from bog oak and of using turf for the homely tasks of fire making and cooking. There is even a type of ancient Irish mousetrap made from a dried sod of turf! What was valued was the hardness that the soft bog brought to the ancient wood that had lain in it for centuries.

There is one tale in which the bog takes a little girl. She comes back to tell her brother how to save her – he must catch her as she rides past the gable of their house on a white fairy horse. But the parents will not allow the child to try to save his sister, in case he too is taken. What are the roots of this story? Does it show a warning against intervention in the business of bog sacrifice?

The year begins in flame. Out of the cold wet wildness, out of the dark that hides and smothers, (and preserves and protects) in the small cottages and after much labour, out of it all came warmth and light. Not a bright dancing flame, but something sullen and slow. The bog goddess warms us.

IMBOLG

Bride put her finger in the river …
And away went the hatching
mother of the cold

Alexander Carmichael,
Carmina Gadelica, 1900

THE FIRST DAY OF SPRING

The first day of February is the feast of Imbolg and Imbolg is the first day of spring in Ireland. It is also the day dedicated to one of the three patron saints of Ireland, Brighid. Spring comes to us early, as if the Irish are either ridiculously optimistic or else intent on celebrating the hidden beginnings of things, the first wavering threads of sunlight, of early thaw. The snowdrop appears, but it often blooms in the snow, for in reality, temperatures still average at around five degrees Celsius, similar to January and slightly lower than December. The winds are still harsh and the ground often remains a sea of mud; water glints everywhere. February can often be a month so cold and miserable that it sometimes feels as if its only real difference from January is the fact that it is shorter. But as the month progresses, the days grow longer and brighter. Imbolg is the time of protection – things hidden, held in before the slow release of spring. Yet the Imbolg season is also the time of the first unfurling and uncovering, the lamb from the mother, the earth from the cloak of frost and snow. Brighid's cloak opens to pull us into safety, to protect us, but also to let us out to new life. This is the slowest, subtlest of times, the time when the stark bare branches become part of a faint haze, a web of small twigs. The haze becomes a mist and as time moves on and the sun grows stronger, there is a slow bursting into bud. And then there will come the day when the trees are covered in tiny leaves. The colours change – very slowly, from dun to the palest of yellow-greens. Towards the end of the season, the first yellow flowers come: celandine and primrose, daffodil and dandelion and buttercup. Spring.

The River Boyne.

THE RIVER'S STORY: BOANN

The Boyne river, which rises in Kildare and flows northwards, forms part of the border between the ancient kingdoms of Ulster and Leinster. It is a river that has played an important role in both history and pre-history. The megalithic monuments of Newgrange, Knowth and Dowth are sited at what is known as Brú na Bóinne (the Bend of the Boyne). Its name comes from Bó Fionn, the Bright or White Cow, and some writers have connected its flow with that of the flow of stars called the Milky Way — in Irish, the Way of the Fair Cow. In the lore, the stars can also be herds of cattle and the shoals of fishes in the sea. Parts of the river were known by other names, such as the Arm and Leg of Nuada's wife, the White Marrow of Fedlimid, the River of White Hazel and the Great Silver Yoke. This again connects it with cows, the yoke that holds the cow-goddess. Venus, in Western astrology, is associated with the astrological sign Libra, whose glyph can be interpreted as both a balance and a yoke. Venus is linked even more suggestively with Taurus, the sign of Bealtaine, whose symbol is the Bull.

Boann became a goddess because of the 'sin' of curiosity. The Boyne was formed when she looked into a magic well. She became goddess of the river, which took her name. The motif of the curious/disobedient woman letting loose the element of water is a common one in Ireland and indeed in Europe. But some questions are left unanswered. Did Boann flee from the water or did she let it submerge her? The maiden becomes a pool of water, the princess becomes goddess; is that really a punishment for disobedience and curiosity? All we can know is that transformation comes to those who take risks.

~

Nechtan was the Master Druid, Keeper of the Well at Segais, sometimes called Connla's Well, sheltered by the Nine Hazel Trees of Wisdom. Their boughs drop their nuts into the water of the well, where they are eaten by a silver fish.

This is the well that may only be seen by Nechtan and his cupbearers, Fles and Lam and Luam. No one else may come near. Certainly not his wife.

***

Why did I do it? Some claimed that I had betrayed Nechtan and needed to wash off the evidence, but that is not the truth. I was a maiden when I went to the well, despite being married. Nechtan was only interested in his well and his cupbearers, who were never out of his sight.

Truth to tell, I was bored and I was curious so one night I went to the well with my lapdog, Dabilla, the creature closest to me in the whole world. I went at the very beginning of the end of winter, when the first green appears through the snow, and the water breaks through and begins to flow from where the ice has trapped it.

I circled it three times and then I looked into it. At first I could see nothing. Then I could see my own face, wavering, the shadow of my hair around it, the moon above me a crescent over my head. And then, clear at the bottom I could see the nuts floating and the silver fish swimming deep, deep below. There was silence except for the call of an owl.

As I watched, the water swirled and pulled my gaze further

down into the depths. And from those depths three waves began to rise, rising, rising, coming towards me as I felt myself being pulled deeper in.

And then the water lifted me, held me, carried me, and now I was afraid. For this was knowledge, beating against me, bearing me along in waves of water, wave after wave. I clutched my little dog to my heart, but could not hold her. The water was too strong.

My foot hit hard against the rocks as the wave rushed onwards. I felt it catch and tear from my ankle and I screamed aloud with the pain, but my voice was drowned in the noise of the rushing water. I left it behind me, the blood flowing, staining the water. My right hand went out to try to hold onto something, to slow my journey, but it was knocked against a tree. I lost it too and watched the blood flow again. In the red flow of blood the silver salmon kept me company.

And now I stopped fighting the flow. I looked beyond the rush of water, watching what we passed. We raced through forests and meandered through pastures. We passed hills and farms and cattle grazing in the sunrise. I caught a glimpse of a fox drinking on the bank of the river, the flow that was taking me eastwards, into the light. He raised his eyes and watched me a moment, then dropped them and drank again. Dabilla flowed with me, an otter-dog. As we travelled past each part of the river, I named it. I saw the river flow through time and the changes on its banks. I saw the great tombs rising, and after that the churches, and after that again the castles and the small thatched houses where the people that came from my people were to live. The river nourished them all.

And then I heard the sound of gulls. Something came from the air and took one of my eyes. I could smell salt water; the warm saltiness that was not blood, not tears, but the sea. This is the end, I thought, the end of the beginning or the beginning of the end. There is no more princess left.

Then there was the final wave, the final crest and falling, into the trough of sleep and forgetfulness. I dream.

Dabilla is still with me. I will be a river and she will be a rock.

I am the river. The river is me. I am Boann.

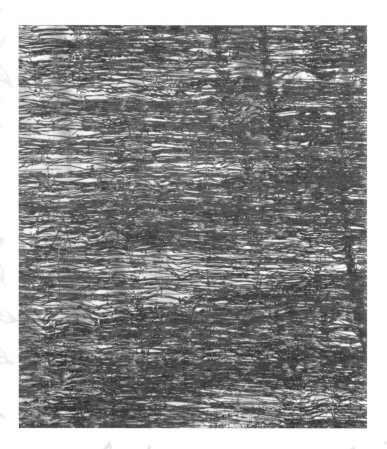

The Festival of Imbolg

As Brigid the Fostermother would smoor
The Fostermother's holy name
Be on the hearth, be on the herd
Be on the household all.

Scottish traditional charm

The festival of Imbolg is interpreted as meaning from the belly, and also in its original form Oimelg, from the word lactation. Imbolg is linked with the spring sowing but its significance is mainly related to the traditions of the herder. This is when the lambs associated with St Brighid and her convent near the Curragh struggle into the cold February world. Brighid is the patroness of domestic animals, the 'Mary of the Gael', whose treasury of folk associations hark back to her former incarnation as a pagan goddess.

The folk traditions associated with the first of February are no longer practised to any large degree, though there have been attempts by Neo-Celtic Christians to revive some of the rituals, and children are still taught how to make the St Brighid's cross in schools. In the 1930s the traditions were still very much alive, especially that of making crosses from wood or rushes. These crosses were hidden in the thatch of the house or hung over a doorway or window. There were numerous forms of this cross, which differed in shape depending on the locality, but some of them, especially in Ulster, had three legs rather than four, and thus reflected the solar wheel and the ocean lord Manannán's triskel.

There was a special emphasis on the cloak or *brat* of the saint/goddess. As the Cailleach's cloak brought winter, Brighid's *brat* brought spring. Brighid is the patron of animals, the keeper of the sacred grove, the healer, the one who weaves meaning into her cloak, a cloak that is light enough to be hung on a sunbeam. So on the last day of January the man of the house would take a cloak outside and leave it to shelter Brighid for the night. On the morning of the first of February it would be taken inside again and would provide protection for the coming year. Sometimes the garment was cut up so that its magical powers could be made available to everyone in the house. The *brat* gained in power as it became older, and was used as a cure for illness and as a charm against dangers such as drowning. It helped women who were trying to become pregnant, and helped them again when they were giving birth. Pieces of the *brat* were also sewn into their daughters' skirts by mothers fearful that the girls would lose their virginity. Fertility, of stock, of crop and of humans, was at the centre of this very domestic festival. Most of the activities were based around the household, hearth and hospitality. A bed was made for Brighid on the eve of her feast day and the door of the house was left unlatched at night so that Brighid and her cow could enter. Food was left out for them, and the fire was left lighted. In some cases a daughter of the house went outside and then came to the door, requesting, as Brighid, to be allowed inside.

But there were also communal activities. Processions of young girls went from house to house, in a custom not unlike the St Lucy's processions of Northern Europe, which took place at the winter solstice and which may have influenced the Imbolg traditions. One of the girls might wear the veil of Brighid and carry her cross and shield; or perhaps she would carry the Brideóg, which was sometimes a doll and sometimes a sheaf of straw kept from the previous summer. Work involving turning wheels was avoided. Carts were not driven, there was no milling or spinning, and even using bicycles and sewing machines was not allowed on this day. All of these reflect solar rituals, and there is a close link between the saint Brighid and her goddess original, who seems to have had strong aspects of a solar goddess of fertility. The solar dandelion is Brighid's flower.

In some localities, the celebrations were marked by groups of young men dressed up as girls, the Biddy Boys, doing the

Biddy Boys.

rounds of the local houses – though even in the 1920s, this tradition was dying out. As at Samhain, the disguises permitted licence – even if everyone actually knew who was hidden under the mask, no one would tell. Eggs and cakes were given to the revellers, sometimes even money. St Brighid's generosity and her hospitality were among her main traits; she no sooner had something than she gave it away and in one poem she wishes for a great lake of ale so that she can offer proper hospitality to the Lord.

Imbolg was primarily an indoor feast – there were no bonfires outside and despite the small processions the bulk of activity was based inside the house. It is closely linked to the Christian Festival of Candlemas on 2 February, which was marked by lighting candles. Candlemas celebrates the Presentation of the child Jesus in the Temple and the purification of the Virgin Mary, the Jewish tradition at the root of the Christian one of 'Churching' new mothers, also essentially a rite of purification. It was celebrated by Christians from the fourth century, though it only took on its strong association with the Virgin Mary much later. In Ireland, it is considered to be a feast celebrating Mary. Candlemas and St Brighid's Day are linked because tradition has it that Brighid hid the Holy Family with her cloak when they were fleeing from Herod's soldiers. The feast of Candlemas is also, in its theme of purification, connected to the Roman festival of Lupercal, although that feast was held later in February. Irish communities managed to hold onto their traditional festival of light and linked it with a local goddess/saint rather than having it subsumed into the more general Christian feast.

Nowhere is the constant melding of pagan and Christian traditions seen more clearly than it is in the figure of Brighid and the traditions associated with her feast day. Even the use of rushes for the crosses has a special significance. Rushes are liminal plants, growing between earth and water. Brighid is associated with water birds, specifically with ducks. The oyster-catcher has as one of its Irish names *Giolla Brighde*, the servant of Brighid. There were practical reasons why rushes were used. They were freely available and easily manipulated into many different forms, including the traditional cross and Brideóg. On a daily basis they were used to make baskets, to thatch roofs, even as buoyancy aids for children learning to swim. They protected and shielded in a very domestic way. They were strewn on the floors of cottages (and indeed in earlier times on the floors of castles) and then swept out of the door when they had become insanitary. There is an old saying: 'If I knew you were coming, I'd shake green rushes for you', because special guests were always honoured by having fresh rushes spread before them in the house. If the house was thatched with rushes, as many were, the household was almost literally wrapped in rushes; protected by having them above their heads and below their feet.

But the most important use of rushes was for light, and for those people who could not afford wax candles stripped rush-lights, dipped in tallow, were an important resource. This linking of fire and light is where the connection with Brighid's day and indeed Imbolg can be clearly seen. Perhaps, long, long ago, the rushes were lit from the fire that was Brighid's holy fire at Kildare, a sacred fire that was kept alight long before the saint came on the scene.

Brighid, the goddess who the poets and craftspeople adored.

Cormac's Glossary/'Sanas Cormaic', *c.* tenth century in Irish

So who was this ancient goddess?

She was a triple goddess, some said the daughter of the Dagda. Her three forms were respectively the patron of healing, of smithcraft and of poetry. She was a fiery goddess, patron of the fire in the forge, the fire of purification that is the beginning of healing, the fire in the head of inspiration. When she stayed in a house overnight, the light was so bright it would appear to be on fire. Her name means 'Exalted One' and she was not solely an Irish goddess – her tribe, the Briganti, held sway in much of central England and she was also found in Gaul, where she was identified with the Roman Minerva. (She also holds echoes of the goddess Vesta, patron of the hearth whose sacred flame was guarded by virgins). Brighid's power of protection was very great, especially over herds and domestic animals. She had two oxen, Fea and Feimhean, who would cry out whenever rape or rapine was committed, emphasising her connection with purity and with protection, especially the protection of young girls. In some of the Scottish Gaelic verses about 'Bride' we see Bride as a white snake, and 'the queen' who 'shall come from the mound' is invoked, the snake sometimes made of peat. This lore hints at elements of the goddess that seems to have been lost in Irish lore. This Irish goddess remains a shadowy figure – mainly because we see her through the prism of the Christian saint.

Long before the time of Brighid the enclosure at Kildare

that became her main convent was already a sacred space, its name, Cill Dara, referring to the oak grove dedicated to the goddess. It has been suggested that the nun who took over as Abbess from Brighid, who shares her feast day and whose name, Darlughdacha, means daughter of Lugh, may have been the original goddess. She may also have been the original of the saint we now know as Brighid, taking the name of the Exalted One as part of her ascent to power. When the monastery was founded no men were allowed in and a fire was kept burning continuously in the enclosure – a tradition that continued until the time of the Normans.

We know much more about the saint than the goddess; indeed the wealth of folklore and legend with her is so great that we can only explore a small part of it. The history of the original girl who founded the monastery and perhaps took the place of the Kildare Exalted One has become encrusted with marvellous stories. She was born c. 439 but was active until c. 524, a very long life for the time. She managed to encounter some of the earlier Irish saints, including St Patrick, and she also managed to travel back in time, to the time of the birth of Christ. She is said to be the daughter of a bondwoman and a druid, and was born in what is now Faughart in County Louth. She was fed the milk of a white red-eared cow, one of the fairy cows linked with the Otherworld. Her Life was written over a century after she died and, like so many of the saints' lives, there was a political end in view, as her importance as a Leinster saint was used to enhance the position of the High King of Leinster.

The Curragh of Kildare, the great plain where herds of sheep are still reared, was her base. When she went to the king to ask for land for a monastery he offered whatever ground her cloak could cover and when she spread it out it miraculously covered the full plain. Brighid's colour was white; and this colour has continued to be the token colour of Kildare, her county. It was worn by the Kildare branch of the eighteenth-century revolutionary group the United Irishmen and much later by the Kildare GAA team, known as the Lilywhites.

Like the goddess Brighid, she was also associated with cows; a cow accompanied her on her visits to the households on Brighid's Eve. Cows start to give more and better milk when

The Irish mantle – Brighid's cloak.

the new grass grows in February. The tradition is that during the winter months the milk goes to the cow's horns. There is an old saying that was used by Irish mothers, when small children had finished drinking their milk, that it was 'All gone to the cow's horn.'

Though Brighid's base was in Kildare, she could hardly have spent much time there. She seems to have never taken a breath, so busy is she, feeding, working, healing, admonishing, protecting. In one story she takes over the churning from her sick mother, the slave, but gives all the butter away. When the master finds this out he is furious, but Brighid manages to magically produce more and better butter. This generosity and emphasis on hospitality makes her an ideal guest at Judy Chicago's *Dinner Party*, an iconic 1970s' installation artwork celebrating female figures through time and space. She was a peacemaker, a healer, and a helper of those in need.

Brighid was also an indefatigable traveller and is often portrayed in her chariot, her charioteer a priest.

In the beautiful poem 'The Clothes Shrine', which constitutes both a very personal love poem to his wife as well as a hymn to the everyday, Seamus Heaney invokes a hard-pressed, unstoppable saint, continually 'on the go'. Brighid, in her various name forms, in later times, needed to be a very hard worker. A *Bridget* was the name given to servant maids in nineteenth-century America, because so many Irish girls were domestic servants. Not all of them were particularly saintly; some turned to a life of crime, usually theft and prostitution, so much so that the New York police created a category of criminal known as the 'Bad Bridgets'.

Decisive, energetic, and yet with a softness about her, the saint succoured wildlife as well as domestic animals, nursing a wild duck and taming the wild boar that rampaged in the woods of Kildare. After her intervention the boar settled down happily as the leader of the herd of tame pigs that rooted for the nuts that fell from her sacred oak trees. In this she is part of a Celtic Christian tradition, in which the early saints become friends of the wilderness and the beasts and birds that inhabit it. St Declan called on the help of a deer to replace a tired horse, St Fintan used wolves as sheepdogs to guard his flocks. It was a peaceable kingdom and the animals protected the saints as the saints protected the animals. St Gobnait's bees became a band of soldiers, their hive a helmet, in order to preserve her from harm.

Later, we will be looking more closely at these connections between the natural world – especially the forest to the saints and hermits of early Irish Christianity. For now, it is enough to say that Brighid was one of a band of saints who befriended and sometimes lived with every animal and bird imaginable, from boars to blackbirds, from sparrows to stags, from wolves to wild ducks. Colmcille, the second Patron of Ireland, shared some of this feeling for nature, though he seems possessed of a quicker temper than Brighid and used his powers to curse on more than one occasion – two women ended up as crows as a result of one of his curses. And when we look at that other member of the saintly trio, the principal saint of Ireland, Patrick, whose feast day on 17 March is the next major day in the calendar of celebration, there is less of a sense of connection to the natural world.

THE FOX'S STORY: BRIGHID'S BARGAIN

There are so many legends about St Brighid's friendships with animals, it is hard to pick one out. But here her relationship with the most maligned of animals, the *madra rua*, the fox, makes for a special kind of story.

~

I am, after all, a fox.

Which doesn't mean that I can't appreciate real goodness when I see it. And even help it along to win the day, if I feel so inclined. Or if I am in debt to it. Just don't go depending on me to do the right thing.

It was probably both debt and inclination which made me help Brighid, that day she came through the wood, belting along the track in her chariot. I was taking my ease in a sunlit glade, the last of the snow melting, snowdrops around me and the soft plash of the stream nearby, when I heard her coming, the noise of the horse through the branches, and her own voice singing. The blackbird that had been keeping me company that morning put his head on one side and sang louder, along with her.

Brighid's voice is as beautiful as her face, with her buttercup locks and her eyes as green as spring grass. She was driving herself, standing tall with the reins in her hands, dressed all in white like something in a dream. To think of Brighid as dreamlike would be a mistake. She may hang her cloak on a sunbeam but she is as full of practical ideas as an egg is of meat. This would be annoying if it wasn't for the fact that most of the ideas she has are plans to help those in need, the hungry, the wounded, the hunted ones. She saved me from a trio of angry farmers once, hiding me in her cloak. When they came along asking her if she had seen me, I found out that she could lie for Ireland. The dogs sniffed around her nervously, unable to get my scent because of the cloak, but sure that I must be somewhere nearby. The men gave up in the end, and I thanked her and said if she ever needed help I would make myself available. Now she was going to call in that favour, not for herself but for the snivelling woman beside her in the chariot.

'I need you to come with me to King Domhnall's dwelling,' she said. 'I have a favour to ask of you.'

'And what has an old fox like me to do with King Domhnall?' I asked.

The woman sobbed harder.

'It seems that this poor woman's husband killed the king's fox,' said Brighid. 'It was a mistake. He thought it was a wild one, not realising that the king had trained it to do tricks to amuse the company at his feasts. Now he says the man must forfeit his life if he cannot produce a fox just as talented.'

So I was supposed to help a fox-killer? What exactly was she asking me to do?

'You want me to …' I paused, letting the indignity of the idea seep into her brain. 'Do tricks?'

Brighid smiled. 'I know it is beneath you, my dear fox, but this is what seems to be needed in this case. This poor woman has travelled for miles to ask me for help.'

'Isn't it all a bit unreasonable of the king?' said I.

Brighid snorted. She can be most unladylike at times.

But then she is not a lady, only a saint. 'When have you ever known King Domhnall to be reasonable?'

I thought about it. I thought about that fat fox-haired bully, his face pale and bloated, storming and shouting during his audiences with the people, lying through his teeth. I reconsidered. Might be no harm to pull one over on him.

'I will come with you to the king and I will do some tricks.' I said. My eyes met Brighid's. We both know exactly what I meant.

At the court, the king was busy eating beefsteaks and tearing the legs off roasted chickens, while the prisoner, tied to a pillar, waited to be executed. His wife ran to him and embraced him, still weeping. What a waste of space that woman was. I was surprised she had had the gumption even to go to see Brighid to ask for help.

Brighid bowed to the king.

He looked up from his drumstick, his face greasy and his eyes clouded with alcohol and said: 'Well, maiden, what is this about?'

Brighid smiled, and lifted her cloak so that the king could see me. I bowed my head. I can lay it on when I need to.

'I understand you have lost a pet fox and this poor man's life is to be forfeit because of it,' said Brighid.

'That is so,' said the king,

'And is there any chance you might show mercy? I understand it was a mistake on the man's part.'

'The fox is dead and there is not a thing you can do about it,' said King Domhnall. 'Unless you can bring it back to life – or replace it with one just as entertaining.'

'I think you will find that this fox will impress you,' said Brighid.

She made a hoop of her hazel staff and I jumped through it; then I rolled over backwards three times and leapt to catch the apple Brighid had plucked from the table and thrown in the air. I didn't eat it though, I held it gently in my jaws and set it gracefully at the feet of the queen, who was sitting beside her husband, draped in cat furs. As always, she was looking bored to death. Her expression never changes. There is a rumour that she has been killed and stuffed.

'Impressive,' said the king, and yawned.

It seemed something more was needed.

Brighid nodded to the musician, who like the rest of the king's servants had to be available to perform whenever the whim for music came upon his highness. He struck up a tune.

I stood on my hind legs and danced a jig. Oh, the humiliation of it. But Brighid was smiling at me. The king was smiling too.

'It is indeed a talented fox. Very well, let the man go, and I will keep your gift, Brighid.'

'You must swear to me one thing, your majesty,' said the saint. She had that steely glint in her eyes now, and the king looked at her with his eyebrows raised. 'You must swear that this man and his wife are free to go now, to come to be my bondsman and woman in the sacred precinct of Kildare.'

'Very well,' said the king. 'Witness my promise, all you who are here. This man and his wife are free from my interference for ever.'

'You have sworn on your oath as a king,' said Brighid.

'I have,' said the king testily, 'I have sworn it and I hold all these here to testify.'

The steel was gone and the smile was back. 'In that case we will take our leave.'

Brighid stroked me gently and said. 'Be good, fox. Enjoy yourself in the court.'

I winked at her.

Well, I had a good dinner of chicken bones that night and I sat in a bondmaid's lap while the musicians played and the court listened to King Domhnall's interminable stories of how he had been cheated out of the High Kingship. But this, I thought, is a hot, sleepy kind of life and it was coming into spring, with a skyful of icy stars and a forest calling. And didn't Domhnall deserve to be cheated, bullyboy that he was? Not so much cheated, really, as tricked. After all, he had taken me on for my tricks.

So when they put me in a wooden pen that evening I dug my way out underneath the palings and was racing through the ferns and back into the forest before you could say *madra rua*.

What did you expect? I am, after all, a fox.

St Patrick and His Day

By the time March comes there is a reddish hue to the land-scape, in the further ripening of leaf buds and the turned earth.. By now there are yellow catkins on the hazels and the first daffodils are out. On pet days, there is birdsong. The rest of the time, there are pewter skies and bitter winds. Yet the days have lengthened noticeably since early January, and there is the knowledge that there, inside the bud of the leaf or flower, growth is coming and there will be bright days ahead. In Ire-land, there were further reasons to rejoice. Weddings were traditionally held during this period, as in the nineteenth cen-tury marriages could not take place during Lent. On Chalk Sunday, the first Sunday in Lent, children chalked the coats

St Patrick's Day.

of men who were still single. It was known as 'Puss Sunday' as many of these singletons were expected to 'have a puss on them', i.e. look disgruntled. On Shrove Tuesday, the day before Lent began, pancakes were made, and in the early nineteenth century young men took part in other less harmless customs, such as cock-throwing. This involved tying a cock to a stake and taking turns to throw stones at it. Whoever killed it could claim it. Hare hunting was also traditionally carried out on this day. Many people gave up drink during Lent as well as engaging in the obligatory fasting, but an exception was made for the national feast day. As it was put so succinctly by one of the schoolchildren in the National Folklore survey, on St Patrick's Day:

> In older times people went to the public houses and got drunk.

National Folklore Collection

> If a fair was held in any place on a St. Patrick's Day, men came home staggering from the effects of drink. This was called "Drowning the Shamrock". The pubs are all closed now on St Patrick's Day.

National Folklore Collection

For many of us with memories of the St Patrick's Day parades of the 1960s and 1970s, with their icy winds, what seemed like endless rain and their swathes of Kelly green, it is perhaps difficult to warm to this celebration and this particular saint. To the schoolchildren of this period he was presented as a stern-faced bishop in full nineteenth-century garb, with snakes crawling through the shamrocks around his feet. As every Irish child knows, St Patrick rid Ireland of snakes and used the shamrock to show how there could be three persons in one God. Except that he probably didn't – it was more likely to have been some kind of wood sorrel, not shamrock, and Patrick was not the first person to bring Christianity to Ireland, though he seems to have been the most successful.

Patrick was a slave child brought from Roman Britain in the fifth century and set to herd flocks on the slopes of Slieve Mish. He eventually escaped from bondage, but was haunted by the voices of the Irish calling him back to bring them news of the true faith. Some of the stories told about Patrick portray him as a less than sympathetic character. This crozier-wielding bishop accidentally pierced the foot of King Aengus while he was being baptised. The poor man said nothing as he thought it was part of the ritual, but it always made me wonder how anyone could stick a spike through someone's foot and not be aware of what was happening.

Patrick is actually a more interesting character than he has been presented to the children of Ireland in the past, a magus not averse to burning and blasting his enemies. He could light up the dark with the glow from his fingers and he battled with demons and with the old gods. He had a trick or two up his priestly sleeve worthy of the druids, changing himself and his followers into a herd of deer so they could make their way safely through a forest where an ambush lay in wait for them. This is why the prayer attributed to Patrick, his Breastplate, is called The Deer's Cry and it calls on the elemental powers in a way similar to the pagan druid Amergin, when he invoked the land of Ireland:

> I arise today, through
> The strength of heaven,
> The light of the sun,
> The radiance of the moon,
> The splendour of fire,
> The speed of lightning,
> The swiftness of wind,
> The depth of the sea,
> The stability of the earth,
> The firmness of rock.

Patrick also lays out his stall in terms of his enemies, asking Christ to set on him a shield:

> Against incantations of false prophets,
> Against black laws of pagandom,
> Against false laws of heretics,
> Against craft of idolatry,
> Against spells of witches and smiths and wizards,
> Against every knowledge that corrupts man's body and
> soul;

We will look again at the magus/warrior aspect of Patrick later, in the chapter on Lughnasa. But the St Patrick of the St Patrick's Day parade still retains a certain grim Victorian demeanour and, despite the virulent green that follows him everywhere, to me he is a relatively colourless figure.

St Patrick's Day

It is important to remember that St Patrick and his feast day are two very different things, for the social construct that is St Patrick's Day was originally very political, grounded in the invocation, not of winds and rocks, but of a firmly Roman Catholic, nationalist Ireland. Which makes it somewhat ironic that the very first celebration (though not parade) of St Patrick's Day was held by Protestants. The first real St Patrick's Day parade was held in Boston in 1737; the first large Dublin parade was not held until 1931.

Like Halloween, there is an element of what is known as the Pizza Phenomenon about the celebration of St Patrick's Day; a custom travels to another culture with the immigrants from the original country, is drastically changed in the new country and is then re-imported back to its original home.

A Victorian cartoon from *The Illustrated London News* shows drunken cherubs cavorting among shamrocks, and the connection of sentimentality, alcohol and the feast day was so marked that almost from the date of the foundation of the Irish State until 1970, the pubs were closed and no alcohol could be sold. Despite the Dublin parade and the many local ones, during these decades the day was one of religious observation, endless Masses echoing to doleful hymns such as 'Dóchas Linn Naomh Pádraig' and 'Hail Glorious St Patrick'.

Throughout the period of the Troubles in Northern Ireland, St Patrick's Day was used as a focus in the United States, in particular, to rally support for Irish Republican cause.

In Ireland, in the early days of the State there was a strongly militaristic flavour to the Dublin parade, but by the 1950s an effort was made to move away from celebrating the military might of five tanks and a landrover, to showcasing Ireland's industry – the scope of which, according to one Pathé commentator at this period, must be a great surprise to many. He also comments on the joys of the pipe band, 'always a thrill for the kiddies', as the film shows some small faces apparently frozen in a rictus of cold, or possibly terror.

This military element in the parades has now been shifted to Easter Monday, another religious feast that has, since Easter 1916, become intermingled with Irish Nationalism. The leaders of the Rebellion were very conscious of the symbolism of the date of their uprising, presenting their probable death as a blood sacrifice for the people. This would lead to new life, in that toxic merging of religious and political feeling that has fed into the ideology of extremists – on all sides – for the last hundred years.

Outside Dublin, there was not a lot more going on than attending Mass. Irish folklorist Kevin Danaher describes the customs associated with the day as meagre. From the late seventeenth century, the custom of wearing crosses of ribbons had existed and this persisted. The boys' and girls' crosses were different, and those made from the old vestments of priests were especially prized. But St Patrick does not visit individual houses, nor does he bless the barns or the animals. Patrick is not attached to the spring soil, though the lambing season is by now in full swing and it was and still is a tradition to have the early crop of potatoes planted by St Patrick's Day. The other side of this purgatorial activity was what went on in the

pubs – the constant drinking and the accompanying maud-
lin sentimentality about the ould sod. So on this day people
ended up sodden, saturated with drink or rain, one way or
the other.

As time went on, further attempts were made to lighten the
atmosphere, to make the Dublin parade less grimly military,
nationalistic and industrial. The Wombles attended the 1976
parade as the Irish Tourist Board began to pour resources into
encouraging Americans of Irish origin to come over and begin
the tourist season early.

By the 1990s the Tourist Board had made a decisive effort
to detach the parade from memories of religious fervour and
bedraggled shamrock. The St Patrick's Day celebrations are
now a full festival, stretching over several days. The focal point
is still the parade, but it is a very different kind of parade,
with impressive floats, carnivalesque monsters patrolling the
streets and a huge range of cultural and indeed multicultural
activities associated with it. A showcase for traditional music
and the arts, it generally brings thousands of people to Ireland,
many of them to enjoy the cultural activities. Many, however,
still just come to be sick on the pathways in places like Temple
Bar, clad in orange whiskers and Leprechaun hats.

Perhaps I should be a little kinder to Patrick and his Day.

Throughout its history it has given a sense of pride to the
Irish abroad, especially when such a sense of self-worth was
badly needed by those who lived in the tenements of American and British cities, where the Irish were very low down the
social pecking order. It was a way to bring the Irish community
together to celebrate the fact of their nationality. And it is quite

an achievement to have one's national day celebrated worldwide, from Montserrat to Monaco. So let's give the bearded bishop his due. It was the inclusiveness of the Irish parades which made them so popular and made St Paddy's day a day to be celebrated internationally. Irish influence in the United States has faded over time, but St Paddy's Day is still a day of festivity there. Perhaps it will be kept alive by the new Irish. Patrick is, after all, the patron saint of Nigeria ... a country which has strong links with Ireland and which is also a major producer of and market for Guinness. But that's a whole other story.

Equinox and Easter

To whom the light birds,
With no soul but air,
All day, everywhere
Laudation sing

'The Praises of God', eleventh-century Irish, translation WH Auden

Hard on the heels of the Festival of Patrick comes the equinox, on or around 21 March, the time of equal day and night. The days after the equinox, when March segues into April, were special days, known as the Borrowed Days and often the time of the last blast of rough weather. It was said that the Old Cow boasted that she could live forever, having survived the month of March, but March, furious at the insult, borrowed three days from April. The cow could not survive the final assault of the wintry storms and died.

If there were rituals associated with the equinox they have

been subsumed into the celebration of Easter, which can happen as early as 22 March or as late as 25 April, though originally, the Celtic Church celebrated Easter slightly later. We have arrived at what, for many, is the most beautiful time of the year in Ireland. If we look at weather patterns it is often the period when the weather is at its sunniest, if not its hottest. Ireland rarely gets scorching Julys or Augusts but it does get wonderfully warm and bright days from late April to early June. Spring flowers and trees blossom; lambs play ridiculous games of chasing and, if you are lucky, you may hear the first call of the cuckoo, making this season the one most associated with the paradise of the Otherworld.

As we have seen, the equinoxes were marked by the pre-Christian communities who built the great stone monuments at Loughcrew. For Christians, the time of the equinox was celebrated as the feast of the Incarnation, nine months exactly before the child, planted into the womb of Mary, is born at Christmas. The annunciation of the coming birth is still marked every day on RTÉ television, although now the tolling bell has become a 'pause for reflection'. The prayer of the Annunciation, the Angelus, was traditionally said in the Catholic households of Ireland at twelve noon and at six o'clock. The transformation from the Angelus to a transmission unconnected with religion is just one example of the changes in Irish society in the late twentieth and early twenty-first century. The influence of religion and religiosity was all-encompassing in Ireland up until the 1990s; from the priestly stations held in country households to the Stations of the Cross on Good Friday.

Easter was celebrated with a range of activities that owe much to a common European tradition. The feast of the 'Son', with the resurrection, has its own rich symbolism which is outside the realm of this book. In Ireland, Church ceremonies created a dramatic build-up to the day, involving almost every day of the week between Palm Sunday and Easter Sunday. Good Friday, the day of the crucifixion, was, in Ireland, a day when time seemed to stand still. Nothing was done except attendance at religious ceremonies; even the pubs were closed. The tradition in Dublin on this day was to visit seven churches – who knows why, although perhaps this was connected to the seven churches of Kevin's Glendalough, which is in the same diocese.

Glendalough.

THE SAINT'S STORY: ST KEVIN AND THE BLACKBIRD

No story encapsulates the close connection between nature and the early saints as much as the one that follows. St Kevin was a sixth-century saint who really did found the monastery in Glendalough, a magical valley in Wicklow. He is reputed to have hated the duties of an abbot and was a misanthrope, even, in a popular song, throwing a woman who annoyed him into a lake. He was a wonder worker, making willows bear apples and a wolf feed a young prince fosterling and, like Brighid, he was generous to a fault. His particular friend was an otter who rescued his psalter from falling in the lake. One of Seamus Heaney's most beautiful poems, 'St Kevin and the Blackbird', is based on the story told below.

~

I was about to fold my fingers over when I felt the soft peck. The light but sharp sensation of claw and beak, the warning call of the mate; the knowledge that a bird had nestled in my palm. But I could see nothing, nor could I move, for I was praying.

People think I'm grumpy. I'm not, I just want to be left in peace. I thought going up into the mountains would do it, and for seven years I was safe, living with the wild things. But then all these disciples came after me and gathered around me and I ended up wearing proper clothes and shoes, with responsibility for a crowd of monks and all the business that goes with that. All the noise of the world, kings begging to send their sons for fostering, prayers and work rotas and buying and selling. And constant questions.

I hated it. Soon there I was, living in a monastery so big that I could not find God in it. I decided it was time to put my foot down about visitors and suchlike, especially the women.

There was one in particular, who had me moidered with questions. The story is that I flung her into the lake, but that is not true. I only turned and tripped her as she was following me, her nose practically up my arse, asking questions, questions. Was I alright? Was I hungry, thirsty, hot, cold, wet? Did I not need her to do something for me? Enough is enough. Now I have a question for you. Was it my fault that the lake was so close?

So I built myself a tiny cell high up on the cliffs, looking over the waters where I could see God again, in the stillness and quiet.

Lent came, and I took off to my cell and said that no one was to come near me. And there I stayed. Every day, long hours of prayer, arms outstretched through the tiny window, for the cell was very small. Total quiet except for the birds. Total stillness in my body. I never felt lonely. Two blackbirds often visited me, a soft brown female and a cheery black fellow with a golden beak. I knew the hares and the otters and the badgers and the fox from the forest. The birds would feed from my hand, the fox would curl at my feet and sleep as the light flickered through the new leaves of the trees.

And then, one April morning, I felt the something. The soft feathers, the hard claws that almost made me clench my hand in fright. It had to be my friends, the blackbirds … but then there was something else on my palm. Leaves, twigs, soft hair from the shedding of the fox and the hare.

A bright, yellow-circled eye met mine through the tiny gap in the stone. The chatter of a couple hard at work. The blackbirds were building their nest. I stayed still, for I was praying. Then, a flurry in the air and soon afterwards something light, and slightly warm, that even on the sole of my palm felt delicate, breakable. The blackbirds sang so loud, so proudly. I twisted my head and blinked against the light of the window. There it was, bright blue-green and speckled brown. An egg laid.

Some people might have thought of breakfast.

I won't lie, the thought did drift across my mind. I had very little left to eat. But I was not going to eat my friend's child, was I? But what should I do? If I moved the egg to another place, the mother might desert it, or I might break it in the moving. So I waited and prayed. And prayed and waited, all through Lent, and the mother came and kept her egg warm. And I like to think the warmth of my body helped as we waited and waited for the egg to hatch. For weeks I stood there and by the end of it my body could not feel itself. I was bird and egg, I was a tree with life hatching in my hands. I was part of the valley and part of the mountain and wind and water and earth, fur and feather and shell.

And finally there was a peeping and a cracking, and after a great deal of palaver, out of the shell came the most miserable, the ugliest looking little fledgling you ever saw.

The bells in the valley below were ringing and the blackbirds sang with delight.

Hare and Egg

I will go into the hare,

With sorrow and such mickle care,

I will go in the Devil's name,

Ay while I come home again

Scottish Traditional Song

The lead-up to Easter Sunday was like a re-enacted passion play, culminating in the Paschal fire of midnight on Holy Saturday.

In popular tradition, on the day itself, anyone up at dawn might see the sun dancing with joy. The eggs that were forbidden during Lent and had been decorated beforehand were eaten and holy wells were visited. Crosses, made from the willow and fir branches blessed in the church the previous Sunday, were placed over doors and windows, and holy water sprinkled in the four corners of the fields. Many parishes held a dance at the local crossroads on the night of Easter Sunday, and some included a competition with a large cake as a prize. Fairs were held on the Monday after Easter. Spring had by now well and truly arrived, and, depending on whether Easter was early or late, the swallows might well have returned to the outhouses. Those other birds, the sparrows and blackbirds and robins, who stayed with us all winter, now had competition for the food resources, but at this stage insect life was also burgeoning so the resources were there. Wild animals had their young and in recent years the Easter Bunny, a construct unknown to the Irish children of the 1930s, brought his chocolate eggs, for the rabbits that the Normans introduced to Ireland did not bring chocolate with them. The children of the 1930s were, however, quite familiar with, and had many stories about, that rather more mysterious creature that is often mistaken for a rabbit – the creature which goes so wild in the spring that the expression 'mad as a March hare' has been coined.

The hare, known to many country people as the little brown cow with no horns, was already present in Ireland in the days when Newgrange was built, as small quantities of bone have been found there. It is associated with the god Donn, the mysterious Lord of the place where the dead go. Although its association with the Saxon goddess Eostre (from whom Easter gets its name) has been challenged, it is a creature that figures in a great deal of both Irish and international folklore, and therefore merits some examination here.

In Scandinavia the hare is the companion to Freya, the goddess of fertility, of growing things, of life. The warrior queen Boudicca offered a hare to Andastre (whose name seems very close to Eostre's), the goddess of victory. Hare bones have been found in sanctuaries in Britain, and also small bronze hares that were obviously offerings.

Ireland has its own species of hare, the mountain hare, which is larger than the lowland version. Famously fecund, the hare can conceive even when pregnant, though spring is its most fertile season and also when male hares can be seen boxing one another. Hares have been associated with witches all over Europe, and could bring either good or bad luck. To have a hare cross your path while pregnant could result in a child being born with what used to be known as a harelip, a cleft palate. Yet a hare's foot is a symbol of good luck, and of healing, a protection against rheumatism. The hare's foot is valued as a charm not just in Europe but also in places far away such as China. The hare would have been hunted for its flesh and its fur, but unlike the deer and the boar does not figure greatly in the Irish sagas. It does figure in the songs and folklore of Ireland, the most common story being that of a hare spotted sucking milk from a farmer's cow. The farmer wounds the hare – either his dog attacks it or he takes a shot at it – and then follows the trail of blood to a cottage. Inside the house he finds no trace of a hare but an old woman, bleeding from a wound. In other versions of this story, fairy hares could only be caught by a black hound, sometimes with white ears. In some parts of Kerry it was once believed that the souls of grandmothers went into hares, and therefore their meat should not be eaten. One theory is that because the mountain hare sometimes uses the lapwing's nest as a bed, and indeed vice versa, it was thought that hares laid eggs – hence the Easter egg, Easter hare/bunny connection. The hare is also very closely connected with the harvest, which will be looked at later, in the Lughnasa section. This animal is also associated with the moon and Easter is a lunar feast, the time of its celebration based on the first Sunday after the Pentecostal full moon.

Eggs, moon, hare and a sun that dances on Easter morning – and the season of Imbolg begins to draw to a close.

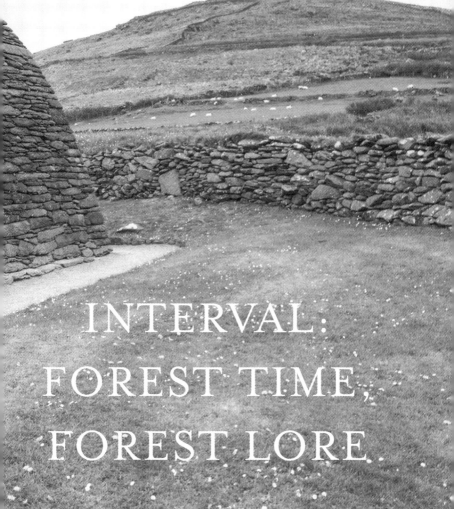

A hermitage that fits my mind
With sun and moon and starlight filled

From a ninth-century Irish poem, *'Inbhir Tuam'*,
translation Robin Flower

INTERVAL: FOREST TIME, FOREST LORE

THE HERMITS

They would be watching from ground level, through narrow windows in thick stone walls, or if there was no window, through the doorway. The forest looked in at the hermits and the men and women who went to the woods to live a life close to God looked back.

Outside was the life of the forest. Inside was the life of prayer. Their rule was that a third of the day would be spent in spiritual exercises, a third in manual labour, and a third in study. As Austin Clarke put it in his translation of the old Irish poem, 'The Blackbird of Derrycairn', knowledge was found among the branches. In the summer the woods would have been dripping with birdsong and the rustling of animals, alive with light shifting through leaves and the sound of water running and the calls of the wild things.

But the stone walls and earth floor meant that the damp didn't just rise: the hermits would have lived with water seeping through the stone and the soil all around them and under them, through their beds of rushes and fern. They had no fireplaces, though they must have lit fires for cooking; their diet was extremely simple and based mainly on the wild things growing around them, nuts and berries and watercress. Much of the time they must have been cold and wet, and let's not even think about the rheumatism of later years. The woods could hold as much discomfort and even danger as the desert hermitages these holy ones were trying to emulate. 'I write well in the shelter of the wood' wrote a hermit-poet of the ninth century; for woods hold their own particular and unique beauty, and in every season it must have been possible to glimpse light through the overarching branches. The monks living in monastic communities dreamed of living in such places and the life lived in these little hermitages are the subject of some of the most beautiful poetry in the Irish language. Some went to desolate islands in the sea or in mountain lakes. But very many walked into the forest.

A hermitage that fits my mind
With sun and moon and starlight filled

From a ninth-century Irish poem, *Inbhir Tuam*,
translation Robin Flower

Science has used dendrochronology as a dating tool since the mid-nineteenth century, and the analysis of tree rings is still used to study past climates and as part of the carbon-dating process in archaeology. The knowledge of the importance of forest cover for the health of the planet as a whole is newer. Even more recent is the development of the scientific knowledge of the life of trees within a forest – how they communicate, heal and feed each other through their root systems and underground networks of fungi, how they co-operate and respond to keep each other alive and in health; the wood-wide web. The collective power of trees to calm us has been popularised in activities such as forest bathing. But long before such ideas became popular, the power of a forest to heal and the comfort given by the feel of branch, bark or trunk was known. The small oak woods, the nemetons where the Celts worshipped,

which may have been the origin of the holy oak groves of saints such as Colmcille and Brighid, the vast forests where Fianna hunted and Mad Suibhne sang with the stag and the blackbird … these are the woods that we have lost.

Clearing the Forests

Ireland is not now, nor has it been for many centuries, a heavily wooded country. The traditional story told to us in school (at a time when history was heavily politicised), was that the English cut down our woods during the Elizabethan conquest, but that is just part of a longer and more complicated process that has resulted in a country that is only 10–11% wooded. When the State was founded that figure was less than 2%, so most of the woods we have are relatively young ones. While great efforts have been made to plant trees, there has been controversy around the type of trees that are being planted, in particular the fast-growing conifers which are death to biodiversity and shroud the hills in parts of counties such as Leitrim. The great native forests only exist in fragments, such as Reenadinna yew wood in Killarney and near

Tinahely in Wicklow. In Reenadinna the trees are approximately two hundred years old, but a forest has existed there for five thousand years.

During the 1930s and 1940s many estate forests, planted in the eighteenth century, were cut and sold by impoverished owners. Previously, in the nineteenth century, great clearances were made for wood to fuel the industrial revolution and the lavish lifestyles of the ancestors of these Anglo-Irish estate owners. The woodlands were cut, according to the eighteenth-century man of letters Horace Walpole, to pay bills at fashionable clubs such as Almack's and racecourses such as Newmarket. Between 1841 and 1881, 45,000 acres of woodland were cleared, sold and not replanted. Prior to that, many of the larger woods had been home to a community of small craftsmen. Derrycunihy, also in Killarney, was the home not just of woodcutters but of colliers, coopers, boat builders, carpenters and turners. The woods would have been alive with the music of their work.

Looking further back, we see that yet more of the woods were razed during Cromwellian times. Others, like the woods at Kilcash in County Tipperary, were sold and used as fuel and timber for buildings and ships.

While the clearance of the woodlands of Ireland is a long sad story, it is true that a significant element in it was the politically motivated cutting down of the forests during Tudor times. The Tudor English hated the forests of Ireland. Particularly during the reign of Elizabeth I there was a campaign of clearing the great, wild woods where the Gaelic rebels had their fastnesses; for it was to the mountains, bogs and forests that the native Irish people went to hide from their invaders. The woods in particular were seen as a refuge for the rebels and were also the most easily removed sanctuary. After raids and sorties or in retreat from a battle, the Gaelic tribes took to the forests, and as they retreated they engaged in plashing, making their route impassable by bending and binding the branches of trees behind them. Thus they created living walls, green citadels.

Yet even the English Tudor poet Edmund Spenser, who described the native Irish as the 'old evil children of the woods', could not resist the beauty of the forests in Kilcolman, his home in Cork. In his wedding song to Elizabeth Butler he describes the Kilcolman woods singing with joy on the morning of their marriage.

> So I unto my selfe alone will sing,
> The woods shall to me answer and my Eccho ring

The Gaelic natives wintered out in the woods, grazing their cattle and pigs on the understorey, safe, hidden by their cloaks, their fringes, their trees. They shared their home with badgers, goats, piglets, deer, foxes – and countless birds.

While the Elizabethan period was one of major clearance, the cutting down had begun long before. By the twelfth century Irish timber – especially oak – had become a valuable commodity which the Normans had already started to cut and clear. Many of the poems celebrating the sanctity of the woodland hermitages were first written down during this period so there may, even then, have been an element of nostalgia for what has already begun to disappear.

The Refuge of the Wood

But there is an immediacy and direct sensory response to nature in these poems that is a far cry from sentimental nostalgia. In these poems we find ourselves immersed in ancient woodlands of oak and ash, of yew and holly and hawthorn, a teeming green sea of all kinds of life, insect, animal, bird and fish. This is the forest of the early saints. Here is a fresh world, a world of joy in creation that carries us back to long before the harsher Catholicism of post-Famine Ireland, a form of religion that looked to punish 'the world, the flesh and the devil'.

Despite the fact that they retreated from society, the Celtic Christians did not share this puritanical world-view. The Celtic saints used their senses – of hearing, sight, touch and smell – to praise God. St Mochua wanders off while a church is being constructed to listen to the song of the blackbird and returns a hundred and fifty years later to find the church long built. Kevin had his Holy Wood (Hollywood in County Wicklow today), Brighid her Church of the Oaks. Colmcille (the dove of the church) swore that in the oakwood of his native Derry (which once again takes its name from its oakwood) the leaves of the trees were filled with hosts of white angels and wrote:

> Though I am fearful, truly,
>
> By death and by Hell;
>
> What frightens me more,
>
> Is the sound of an axe in Derry in the west.

> Manus Ó Domhnaill,
> 'Vita Columbae', seventeenth century

As we have seen, the relationship of the saints and animals was a very close one, so close, in fact, that at times the animals became human and the humans animals. A blackbird, singing on the gable end of a hermitage, is hailed as a cloaked woman. A boar was St Ciaran of Saighir's first monk. St Ailbe hid a she-wolf's head in his cowl when she came looking for refuge from hunters. St Maedoc fed a number of hungry wolves in his time and on one occasion he gave a calf to a wolf. When the calf's mother lamented her child he made her lick the head of one of his monks, who became a substitute for the lost calf. In many cases the animals were given a task: St Ciaran had a fox carry his missal to church. Then there were the beasts that showed the way; a flock of white deer guided St Gobnait to where she was to build her church and keep her soldier bees in Ballyvourney in southwest County Cork.

In the stories and poems of this time, invocations are made to the creatures of the forest, to the blackbird guarding her brood in a bothy in the wood, to the grey-cloaked cuckoo, to the dog fox with his white stockings. There is no arrogance in the poems and no complacency or self-centred posturing, no sense of the human being greater or 'other'. The poem where King Guaire speaks with envy of the life of his brother, the hermit Marbhan, is a perfect example of the dream of escape to the greenwood, to the ivy-covered cell that is a peaceable kingdom. Another poem, attributed to the seventh-century saint Manchán, begins:

> I wish, O Son of the living God, O ancient eternal King, for a hidden little hut in the wilderness, that it might be my dwelling. An all-grey shallow water beside it, a clear pool to wash away sins through the grace of the Holy Spirit. A beautiful wood close by, surrounding it on every side, for the nurture of many voiced birds, for shelter to hide them.

Birds appear again and again in the poems, their song a background and aid to trance-like prayer. The hypnotic states brought on by constant chanting and those created by watching or listening to the rhythms of the natural world are similar in their effects. Light on water, light through leaves, the pattern of bare branches intersecting with each other, drawing our eyes upwards, can all create a state of mind that is close to trance, and a sense of peace that, centuries later, Irish poets still searched for. This is what WB Yeats was seeking when, desperately homesick, he stood looking at a fountain in the window of a shop in London, dreaming of the peace of his 'Lake Isle of Innisfree'.

The branches of the forest trees, reaching upwards and interleaving, pulling us into their maze, are also found in the manuscripts of the scribes, which very often have small animals peering through, as do the carved stone branches of the ceilings of Gothic cathedrals. Some of the nature poems survive in hiding, written on the margins of the manuscripts the monks worked on. Many have the simple, subtle power of a haiku:

> Such a lovely day
> I pause to let the sun's rays
> Illuminate my page.

This intense closeness to nature did not spring naturally from the teachings of Christianity, whose desert fathers looked out on a much more hostile and arid landscape. It is a legacy of the Celtic heritage of nature poems and stories set in nature – the hunts of the Fianna, the flight of Mad Suibhne through the branches, the praises of summer, of winter, of every season's glory.

Sacred Trees

In the ninth century the *Triads of Ireland* noted that the three 'nurses of theft' were darkness, a wood and a cloak, so woods could also be perceived as places of danger, as could certain trees.

To the Celts, individual trees were held as sacred, in a tradition that lives on today, both in the 'lone tree' associated with the Otherworld and the Holy Trees that are found beside holy wells, often festooned with pins and rags, with pleas for intercession.

In early Irish history, trees were also associated with individual tribes, and an attack on a tribal tree, the Bile, was taken as an attack on the safety and wellbeing of the tribe itself. This Bile had sacred status and such a tree was sometimes used as an inauguration site for kings and acted as a protector of the territory of the tribe. The Great Trees of Ireland are listed in the Annals: the Ash of Tortu, the Oak of Mugna and the Yew of Ross. Trees were also associated with the Otherworld and with magic: magic apple branches lured Connla to the Land of the Sídh and made Cormac forget his daughter, his son and his wife. A hazel rod was often used for transformation and was also the club carried by ceremonial messengers. In Celtic lore each tree had individual characteristics, and could be a noble or a commoner of the wood. Apple trees were associated with the Otherworld, hazel with wisdom, acorns with kingship. The fire and flame of alder rods were used to see the future. Holly was used for spears; ash for chariots. The Ogham alphabet, the earliest Irish writing, is based on symbols for the various trees of the forest.

There is a story in the *Senchas Már,* where Fionn meets the exile, Derg Corra in a forest. It encapsulates the magic of the Celtic woodland: Kuno Meyer translates:

One day as Finn was in the wood seeking him [Derg Corra] he saw a man in the top of a tree, a blackbird on his right shoulder and in his left hand a white vessel of bronze, filled with water, in which was a skittish trout, and a stag at the foot of the tree. And this was the practice of the man, cracking nuts; and he would give half the kernel of a nut to the blackbird that was on his right shoulder while he would himself eat the other half; and he would take an apple out of the bronze vessel that was in his left hand, divide it in two, throw one half to the stag that was at the foot of the tree, and then eat the other half himself. And on it he would drink a sip of the water in the bronze vessel that was in his hand, so that he and the trout and the stag and the blackbird drank together.

Then his followers asked of Finn who he in the tree was, for they did not recognise him on account of the hood of disguise which he wore. Then Finn put his thumb into his mouth. When he took it out again, his Imbas illumines him and he chanted an incantation and said: ''Tis Derg Corra son of Ua Daigre,' said he, 'that is in the tree.'

This is a mysterious and powerful image, like something from the Gundestrup Cauldron, invoking earth, water and air. The elements are held together by the seer in the tree, who shares the nuts of wisdom, the magical otherworld apples and the water of life with his companions of the wood.

Even before the time of the Celts, the forest clearances were starting, and creating problems that are still with us today, as happened when the pine forests were cleared for the Céide

Fields. And now, in our attempts to deal with the climate crisis we have brought on ourselves, we are planting trees. But this brings its own problems. In places such as Leitrim, over the years there have been objections to the mass planting of species such as the Sitka spruce, a fast-growing conifer that kills biodiversity on the land it covers. These dead woods are being used to offset fines payable for the carbon emissions of cattle herds. There is a greater consciousness now of the importance of planting native hardwoods and more support from the State for this, but even still, only 2% of the forest cover of Ireland is made up of native species, our natural calendars of climate and change.

Our ancestors looked at the forest and the forest looked back. In the ninth-century poem already mentioned, Marbhan the hermit tells his brother King Guaire of the wild things that come to his home in the wood. The badgers and deer and wild goats, a 'great host', peaceably assembles outside his hut, gathering, folding him in, as the trees around him shelter and hold him safe.

BEALTAINE

Wild and gay, the blackbird's song

Fionn's poem 'In Praise of May'

SUMMER SEASON

May doll, maiden of Summer,
Up every hill and down every glen,
Beautiful girls, radiantly dressed,
We brought the Summer with us.

Bábóg na Bealtaine, maighdean an tSamhraidh,
Suas gach cnoc is síos gach gleann,
Cailíní maiseach go gealgáireach gléasta
Thugamar féin an Samhradh linn.

Traditional Irish song

By the first of May, the light gathers and holds. May Day, in Irish Lá Bealtaine, heralds the bright half of the year. For many, this is Ireland at its loveliest, with its haze of green growth, scudding clouds and light filtering through young leaves or shining on rushes reflected in water. No more hunkering down, hiding inside; the swallows swoop over our heads, so fast that we are hardly aware of them before they are gone; the cuckoo has returned and every hedgerow and tree is alive with young birds and their songs. Walking the fields, it feels as if every tree has a voice. But the human return to the world outside brings risks and must be managed, acknowledgement made and tribute paid to the dark that will, inevitably, return.

Lá Bealtaine is the second great divide in the traditional Celtic calendar, and a time of great power; a seedbed of potential good and bad luck. The name of the festival comes from *tine*, which means fire and from *Beal*, who is sometimes identified with the Celtic god Belenus, the shining one. In modern times the month of May itself is dedicated to the Virgin Mary, a tradition which brought its own customs and rituals to Ireland. But May Day itself figures strongly in Irish mythology. Lá Bealtaine is the day when Parthalon landed at Kenmare in Kerry. He was the leader of one of the first groups of people to come to Ireland, sometimes said to come from Spain, sometimes from Greece. His people prospered in Ireland, until all of them died in a single week – ten thousand people killed by a mysterious plague that also arrived on May Day, again emphasising the sense of threat as well as celebration that is integral to the festival. Lá Bealtaine is not a comfortable time. It is a passageway, a portal between the world of summer and winter, and portals do not let only good things through to our world.

SKETCHES FROM IRELAND : SPINNING NET THREAD IN THE CLADDAGH, GALWAY.

THE CAT AND DOG'S STORY: THE HORNED WOMEN

I love these mysterious horned women and their flight back to the magical mountain of Slievenamon — the Hill of the Women. This story was collected by Lady Wilde in the nineteenth century, with one or two variants found in the National Folklore Collection. I first came across it as a child in one of the Andrew Lang's Fairy Books, which had a marvellous picture of the Horned Woman, while the phrase 'My blood is on the lips of the sleeping children' always managed to send shivers down my spine. Foot water was used to wash the feet at night time, an important task if you had been going through mud and worse in your bare feet during the day. It was never to be kept in the house or even in a pail outside the door, but had to be thrown away from the house. There were no doubt very practical hygienic reasons for this activity, but it also holds the echo of the old tales, such as that of Nera.

~

There was a house on a hillside, and a fine house it was. The farm around it was fertile and the beasts and the fields and the trees were well looked after. There was a woman, the woman of the house, and she was a very lazy woman. She preferred to be out with the birds and the animals than looking after her house and doing her jobs indoors. She neglected doing all the work that needed to be doing, like cooking and cleaning and spinning and weaving. She had us to keep an eye on her, the Cat and the Dog of the household, but she was a stubborn woman and went her own way. She had three children and a husband who had to go away sometimes, to bring the cattle to the fair in the town on the other side of the valley. She would watch for his return, standing in the shade of the hazels and looking across the river valley, where in the distance she could see the slopes of Sliabh na mBan, the Mountain of the Women, the fairy mountain. We would sometimes go out with her, for it's the job of the dog to guard her humans and the job of a cat to make sure that they are not up to badness.

There was one bright evening, when her husband was away and the woman had been watching the clouds pass over the fairy mountain all day. Then she had watched the sun set the mountain ablaze as it went down in the west. Then she said goodnight to the birds and creatures of the hillside and went inside to her children and put them to bed. She looked at their clothes and realised that they were too small for them and full of holes. So she began to work. Everyone knows that spinning should be done when the sun is passing through the heavens, in the daytime, while knitting should be done at night when the sheep are asleep. But this woman spun and she sang. She was so intent on the work that although we both warned her, with growling and with prowling, with staring and with scratching, with whining and with barking, that she had not put out the dirty water she had washed her children's feet in, she paid no attention to us and neglected to do so.

That is what brought the witches on her. There she was, spinning by firelight and candlelight, and singing away, when there was a great knocking at the door.

'Who is that?' she called.

A deep voice said: 'I am the woman with one horn.'

The knocking continued, growing louder and louder until the woman was afraid it would wake the children. She went and opened the door. Standing there was a big tall woman with red hair that reached her feet. On her forehead was a huge, curving horn. She entered straight away and began to card wool, working in a mad rush. She said nothing and the woman thought — well, if she wants to help me, I'll let her be.

They continued like this until the big woman said: 'Where are they? Why are they late?'

The woman of the house was just about to ask who she meant when there was a banging on the door.

'Who is it?' she said.

'It is the woman with two horns' came a voice from outside.

The first woman opened the door and in came a big tall woman with two horns on her head. She had a spinning wheel in her hand and she began to spin wool. And so it went on, for a third woman came, this one with three horns on her head, and another one with four, until the moon had risen, and crowded around the fire were twelve big women, and the last of all had twelve horns on her head. They spun and carded and wove, and the woman looked at the horns on them and was afraid.

And then they said to the woman of the house: 'We are hungry, make us a cake!'

The woman of the house was very fearful at this stage, for her house was crowded out and the women seemed settled forever by her fireside. So she said: 'I need water for that, and I have none.'

'Take a sieve and get water from the well,' commanded the woman with twelve horns.

The woman of the house did not want to leave her children with these strange creatures, but the women looked at her so angrily that she did what she was told. She took her sieve and went out into the moonlight and walked to the well, which stood between two hazel trees. We went with her to see what would happen.

Of course the water would not stay in the sieve. So she sat and cried, for she was afraid to return to the women with no water. And she was afraid that they might take her children from her, for although she was a careless housewife, she was a loving mother. She looked at herself looking back at herself in the water of the well, with the moon behind her head like a silver halo and her tears dropped into the water. Then a voice from the well said: 'Cover the bottom of the sieve with yellow clay and moss, and it will hold water for you.'

So the woman did that, and scooped some water from the well, and stood up, ready to take her water back to the house.

Then a voice from the branches of the hazel tree said: 'When you return to the house, call out that the Mountain of the Women is on fire.'

The woman of the house went back to the cottage. She opened the door and called out: 'The Mountain of the Women is on fire!'

Inside the house a terrible wailing and lamentation broke out, and the twelve horned women rushed out by her, tearing at each other in their hurry. And they took flight over the fields towards Slievenamon, crying that their children would be burnt.

When the woman of the house went into the house, I, the dog, said to her: 'There are four things you must do to keep the witches away.

'First, you must sprinkle the footwater over the threshold.'

'Then,' said I, the cat, 'you must take the cloth they have woven and place it half in and half out of the chest; and then you must secure the door with rowan and holly.'

And, I, the dog, continued, 'You must bake a cake with the blood that the women have spilled in their rush to get out of the house and break it up and place it on the lips of your sleeping children.'

And this time, the woman listened to our advice and did exactly what she was told.

She had hardly placed the last crumbs of the cake on her children's lips when she heard howling and screaming outside. The witches were back. They rattled on the door that she had bolted and locked and then as one they called out: 'Open, feet water!'

'I cannot,' called the water, 'for I am spilled.'

And then they screamed: 'Open, door!'

'I cannot,' said the door, 'for I am fixed with rowan and holly.'

'Open!' They shouted. 'Cake, that holds our blood!'

'I cannot,' said the cake, 'for I am broken and crumbled and my blood is on the lips of the sleeping children.'

And the witches had to fly back to Slievenamon and leave the woman and her family in peace.

It is said that the mantle the horned women made and left behind them was kept by that family for hundreds of years afterwards. Whatever the truth of that, it is sure that the woman of the house was more careful about not spinning at night and remembering to throw dirty water out of the house before darkness, ever after that terrible night. But we are not going to tell you whether she worked any harder in the house or stopped looking over the hills to the Mountain of the Women as the evening sun went down. She is a kind mistress and we can both keep a secret.

The Festival of Bealtaine

The first of May is celebrated all over Europe, especially in its northern countries. In Germany and Scandinavia bonfires are lit on the eve of the first of May, the Feast of St Walburga, traditionally associated with protection from witchcraft. In the Czech Republic, Marzanna, the old hag of winter, is symbolically burnt on a hilltop fire at around this time. In *The Golden Bough*, the anthropologist James Frazer records a ceremony celebrated in the Tyrol, that involved fumigation by juniper and rue and a great deal of noise, including banging pots and pans and ringing church bells. Fionn's poem to May, written in the seventh century, tells us: 'Weak is the man who fears

noise' – and the instinct to make noise to drive away fearful things is a very deep one, perhaps because when one's ears are full of noise one cannot think or feel enough to be afraid.

Writing this in 2020, one thinks of the people who went out to cheer their health workers every evening, banging pots and pans and making as much noise as possible. Were other, hidden needs met by this group cacophony? In some traditions snakes were also reputed to come out of the ground on May Day and they too were driven away by the loudest noises possible.

Beliefs and Traditions of May Eve and May Day

On May Eve and May Day, there was an emphasis on staying close to home and avoiding mischief, keeping away from the raths and lonely places where the 'Good People', as the fairies were called, might be engaged in their own business of celebration and might not take kindly to anyone spying on them. Which begs the question of what did go on between them and those who braved these places and were rewarded with the gift of privacy. But Lughnasa, not Bealtaine, was the courting festival and the month of May was considered to be an unlucky one for marriages, despite the natural fertility of the month.

As at Halloween, it was not a good idea to be out after dark, or even in the evening on May Eve. The darker and more fearful side to the Celtic celebrations trickled down to the piseogs of Irish farm life, many still in place in mid-twentieth-century Ireland.

Churn and cradle were especially at risk from interference by the Good Folk on May Day, and both were often hung with yellow flowers or red rags to keep harm away. In order for life to move forward, certain actions had to be taken to protect the young growing things. Bealtaine celebrates the time of growth, the summer months, and the traditions associated with it are rooted in the land, especially in activities associated with cows and milk. It was also, as reflected in its name, a fire festival, and bonfires played a significant part in the celebrations in Ireland as well as in those of its northern neighbours. In ancient times cattle were driven between two bonfires in order to protect them from disease during the coming year. By the time of the Folklore Project, cattle were not driven through the fires but singed with a wisp of burning straw. Sometimes protection took the form of tying a red rag to the beasts' tails, a custom that came to be seen as a bit of fun by the children of the household, if not necessarily appreciated by the cows themselves.

May Eve and May Day were also times when nothing could be given out of the house, especially milk, for it could be used against the giver. (Milk was, however, sometimes left out on that night for the fairies – they were inordinately fond of milk and liable to steal it otherwise). Spending money was discouraged, as was borrowing or lending any household or farm item. Wheels were not turned, for travelling or spinning; nothing was washed in running water. Conversely, good luck could be brought to the house by being the first to get water from the well on May Day morning; freckles could be cleared by washing in the morning dew; and health boosted by gathering certain herbs. Some of the customs intermingled protection with celebration; windows were decorated with flowers and green branches and rowan was hung over the doorways to guard against the Sídh.

The red-berried rowan was considered a very lucky tree in Irish folklore, with many healing and protective properties, and its Irish name *caorthann* comes from the word *caor*, that can mean berry but also means flame, again linking the element of fire, and the colour red to this celebration.

The other tree with strong links to the fairies, the whitethorn, the maybush, was put up at the door and sometimes decorated with the remains of brightly coloured Easter eggshells.

These May Day traditions were not confined to rural areas. In the eighteenth-century Dubliners hung out their maybushes, held bonfires in the Liberties, the Coombe, Smithfield and Bully's Acre at Kilmainham and raised maypoles at Finglas and Harold's Cross. They also decorated carts and carriages with green branches. Hawthorn, with its creamy, heavily scented May blossom, was widely used, but while it was hung outside it was never brought into the house.

As we have seen, the colour red was also important. Because

of its connection with both fire and blood, it was widely used, as in the red flannel ribbons tied to cows' tails. Red flannel was a ubiquitous charm; used for earaches, swellings, rheumatism and to keep off colds in winter. There has been a song written about the power of red flannel, not a century or even fifty years ago, but in 2017. The song, by the Dingle singer Eilís Kennedy, tells the true story of how a travelling woman advised her great-grandmother to sew a piece of red flannel into her husband's shirt, to protect him from drowning when he was fishing out at sea. When the woman made the mistake of admitting what she had done in Confession, the priest told her to take the charm away. Very soon after she had done so, her husband was drowned, close to the shore while bringing a huge catch of mackerel home. But in contrast to this Kerry priest, in some cases the Church itself was actively involved in promoting red flannel as a charm, on St Blaise's Day, 3 February, blessing pieces of it in the churches of Dublin for the protection of the throat. The difference, no doubt, lay in the person proposing the charm; an old travelling woman would be linked with superstition and the powers of darkness, the priest with the intercession of the blessed saints.

Blood was also connected with some of the earthier, primitive rituals of May Day. In the nineteenth century there are accounts of cattle being bled in a local rath on Lá Bealtaine and menstrual blood was sometimes mixed into a bed of hay as a counter-charm to cows being 'overlooked' by the fairies. Rotten meat, rotten eggs and other decayed items were also used in these piseogs, most of them buried in places where if nothing else, they would rot and create a terrible stench.

On a brighter note, as well as red ribbon, the yellow flowers that begin to appear around this time were tied in bunches to the tails of the farm animals for protection. Buttercups, primroses, marsh marigolds and the flowers of the broom and furze also decorated windows and doors and were hung over wells. May Day was the day when fairy women or witches, in the form of hares, would be most likely to come to suck the milk of cows left out overnight. So the boundaries of the fields were protected by more yellow flowers, or sometimes by rowan.

May Day is no longer celebrated by the country people of Ireland in any meaningful sense. According to some accounts, the last bonfires were held during the first quarter of the twentieth century, dying out during the troubled times of the War of Independence and the Civil War. In the twenty-first century, even the more recent Christian manifestations of the ancient May Day celebrations have faded somewhat. In the parlance of the church, May Day is the Feast of St Joseph the Worker. But a spring festival at this time of year goes back to

Roman times, when the feast celebrated the goddess of flowers and new growth, Flora. During the Floralia, women of
easy virtue played an integral part in the festivities and our
familiar friend the hare, symbol of fertility, was released as
part of the ritual games. These traditions are mirrored in the
'going a Maying' of the Middle Ages, where young people
rode out into the greenwood and got up to a lot more than
gathering flowers. In Ireland, flowers were gathered for a very
different purpose, to honour the Christian symbol of purity,
Mary, Mother and Virgin.

May Altars

When I was a child growing up in rural Dublin in the 1960s,
in the family home and in school a May altar, festooned with
flowers, was made and the church held a May procession,
honouring Mary. May altars are still made in some homes
and schools and if nothing else, they are a very beautiful celebration of the return of the summer, of green growth and
flowers. May altars have their origin in nineteenth-century
Italy. Like Italians, Ireland's people felt a strong emotional
connection with the Mother of God, the female face of the
Deity. During the nineteenth century, the cult of Our Lady of
Lourdes became hugely important to the Irish and continued
into the twentieth century. A Lourdes holy water bottle with
a bright blue screw-cap crown and roses at her feet generally held pride of place on the May altars made by little girls.
This plastic Queen of Heaven was surrounded by candles and
jam jars of cowslips, bluebells, late primroses and sometimes,

though rarely, early roses, for these home altars were mainly decorated with flowers from the fields and hedgerows rather than gardens. Churches had more formal and elaborate May altars and May processions were held well into the 1960s, with last year's crop of First Communionites, robed in white, walking dutifully behind the statue of the Virgin.

One National Folklore Collection story throws a different light on the common assumption about Mary's mildness. It tells of how a May procession in Mullingar took a bad turn: a woman dressed her Pomeranian in a blue cloak and mocked the procession as it went past. A year later, on the eve of the May procession, the woman gave birth to a child – a perfect little boy, except that he had a dog's head.

Sometimes the statue of Mary was crowned with flowers; 'Queen of the Angels/ And Queen of the May' as the Marian hymn went – again, perhaps an echo of the May Queen, an English tradition with very few parallels in Ireland. Before the May Queen in Ireland became Mary, she was, as we have seen, the maybush.

> Another old custom is the making of a Maybush on May Eve. A nice thorn bush is cut and is decorated with bunches of flowers, ribbons and sometimes lighted candles. The children carry it around from house to house singing Hymns. Then they place it in a hedge to welcome in the May morning.
>
> National Folklore Collection

The May blossom of the hawthorn, though it blooms in late

May in Ireland, is never used on the May altars for it was considered a fairy plant. If the hawthorn is interfered with, bad luck and sometimes even death might follow. This is especially the case of the lone bush, those single trees usually bent crooked by the prevailing winds that dot the small fields of the west of Ireland. Although hawthorn was associated with dark magic it was also sometimes, like the rowan, planted or placed over house entrances to keep witches away. It is also very often the tree associated with holy wells. Its reputation may have something to do with the fact that it is fertilised by flies but also perhaps because of the intransigent nature of the tree itself. It's an effective, fast-growing field barrier – no animal is going to push its way through the thorns of a hawthorn hedge, as anyone who has ever had a close encounter with one will vouch.

Pentecost

Like Samhain, May Day was also what was called a Gale Day, when half a year's rent must be paid and tenancies were begun or ended. Servants were hired for the summer months at the fairs. The calves had been weaned and cows were moved to mountain pastures to stay for the summer months. The world opened up, travelling was easier and the days were moving towards their longest and brightest period of the year.

Many of the traditions associated with May Day in Ireland are celebrated a little later in parts of northern Europe, at Pentecost or Whit Sunday. Pentecost is celebrated fifty days after Easter, so it can fall any time between mid-May and early

June. In Ireland there were no celebrations on Whit Sunday; indeed, it was considered one of the unluckiest days of the year. Rivers and lakes were avoided as to go near water on this day was to risk drowning, for water became evil and would pull you under. Any creature, be it calf, foal or a human child, born on the day was said to be unlucky or would go to the bad, perhaps even becoming a killer or being killed. The children born at Whitsun were known as Cincíse or Kinkisha from the Irish word Cincís, meaning Pentecost. The Halls, when they visited Ireland in 1836, were told that the only thing to do with a creature born during the three days around Pentecost was to *scraw* them – bury them and then dig them up, to get rid of the old bad thing; for after being born again from the earth it becomes a new thing. If this is not done, blood will be shed by the child or beast, even if it is that most placid of creatures, a cow. Other ways to negate the bad fortune of a Pentecost birth involved placing the child in an open grave for a few minutes. If you baulked at burying your newborn baby, there was one other way to stop such a child from becoming a murderer. This was to put a worm or small bird in the baby's hand and fold your own hand over it to make it crush it to death.

Fairies and Piseogs

O heart the winds have shaken, the unappeasable host
Is comelier than candles at Mother Mary's feet.

WB Yeats, from 'The Unappeasable Host'

Some see Whitsun as having taken on the darker, more negative features of May Day. As on Lá Bealtaine, the piseogs sometimes involved burying nests of raw meat, rotten eggs and menstrual blood in the neighbour's haystacks to bring them bad luck (or at least a very nasty swarm of flies). Human tricks, like catching out the changeling by boiling water in an eggshell or wearing your coat inside out were important ways to contain the threat of these otherworldly beings.

Some of the methods used against the fairies could be savage. Witness Bridget Cleary, killed by her husband and relatives in rural Tipperary in 1895 in an attempt to bring back the 'real wife', so convinced they were that a changeling had taken over her body. Not so lethal but equally disturbing was the casual cruelty recounted in less savage stories. To get back their own child, parents often risked killing the misshapen and puny creature the fairies had left in its place. These children were placed on hot shovels, left naked on the side of the road, held with their heads underwater. Like the witch trials, which mercifully did not take place in Ireland, these activities held an element of sadism and perhaps had the ulterior motive of removing the weakest elements of the community. There were various degrees of cruelty inflicted in getting rid of the changeling.

In one account a child takes to her bed and wastes away; everyone is convinced the fairies have taken the real child and left one of their own in her place. Then one day a drunken traveller comes to the house and is given food by the fire. The child's mother goes outside and the drunk starts to roar at the sick child, addressing it as a changeling. He tells it: 'I'll burn you, I'll scald you, you are only blackguarding, get out and go to play – there's nothing wrong with you.'

Terrorised, the 'changeling' goes out to where the other children of the household are playing, and in the words of the story: 'the right child walked in after about ten minutes.'

The Otherworld could be used as a form of social control, not always as cruelly as in the above story, but as a way of keeping children away from people and places that could be dangerous to them.

The Sídh of these May Day tales and indeed the púcas, banshees and even the less frightening but still malicious leprechauns are a very far cry from the fluttering, pastel fairies of Victorian children's stories. It is also interesting that Irish fairies do not seem to have engaged in the helpful household tasks that the hobgoblins of England did; they are not domestic entities. Rather, it was believed that keeping the house and byre clean and performing tasks such as throwing out the foot water at night would keep them at bay. Various stories tell of their origin; they were seen as fallen angels, Eve's children, cruel creatures who cared nothing for human woes. Their habitats were the ancient structures, the dolmens and raths that dotted the countryside and much of their ancestry lies in the original gods of the mounds. Some of them, such as Áine, the Fairy Queen of Munster, are directly connected to the gods and goddesses of the ancient Irish.

As we have seen, the fairies were also known as the Good People, the Gentry, but the desire was still to keep them at bay. The use of the word for fairies, *síoga*, was forbidden if you suspected their presence. And yet these creatures, the Sídh from the fairy mounds, are also beautiful and gay and enchanting.

For author and oral historian Angela Bourke, the fairy house, rath or fairy fort acts as a kind of retrieval code to a wealth of hidden knowledge, some of it now lost. Thus the Sídh, or fairies, link us with our ancient past and also with nature and the landscape. A sudden swirl of wind was a fairy troop going by. A strange crying sound in the night might well be a banshee. The disappearance of a pretty girl or a strong young man for a short period might be because they had gone to dance and feast or play hurling with the Sídh. As they were very fond of dancing and music, the Sídh often stole fiddlers and pipers to play for their revels. The trick was to let no food or drink pass your lips, or you would be trapped in the fairy mound. But if a musician was very lucky, he might come back with the tune that would have fairy magic in it. The fairies were also extremely territorial; they liked to keep their hurling fields and hills to themselves, as one group of girls who visited Knockainey in Limerick one St John's Eve (23 June, the eve of the feast day of St John the Baptist) were told in no uncertain terms. But these otherworld beings had no qualms about invading human space themselves.

The Pooka.

THE PUBLICAN'S STORY: THE PÚCA

The mischievous púca, or pooka, most commonly appeared as a black horse but sometimes as a large black dog. In some of the accounts found in the Folklore Collection the púca was an even stranger creature. It could be half pig, half wolf, half pony, sometimes a goat and sometimes a ghost, and sometimes even a suspicious human, man or woman; usually one who was reluctant to let their face be seen in public.

There are connections between the púca and the Gíle Deacair, the grey horse who carries humans to the otherworld. Púcas are somewhat malicious and their favourite trick is to bring unsuspecting humans for wild rides all around the countryside, through brambles and briars, usually dropping them in a bog hole. They may also guard treasure and their painful and frightening but never fatal rides are often used to teach a lesson to those who have been threatening fairy places. The púca is closely associated with Halloween, although it could appear at any time of the year and there is an account from Glin in Limerick of those attending midsummer bonfires leaving early so that the Púca would not get them. In a story retold by the antiquary Thomas Crofton Croker, set on May Eve, 'Peggy' foolishly stays out after dark and has an encounter with a strange black goat with long wide horns. Standing on its hind legs it stares down at her from the top of a stone wall. When she takes flight, it pursues her and jumps onto her back, only letting her go when she remembers to bless herself three times. The story that follows is an amalgam of some of these themes, brought forward to more recent times.

~

'He'll have a right head on him tomorrow.'

As he spoke, Peadar jerked his head in the direction of Tom Hanly, who had been making serious inroads on my stock of whiskey these past three hours.

I checked that Hanly wasn't looking our way and nodded. 'He certainly will.'

I am going to have to refuse him, I thought, if he looks for more. He's not a good-natured drunk, Tom Hanly. He was already muttering loudly into his drink about the shite music that was being played by the lads in the corner. I sighed and moved to his end of the bar, ready to have a word.

But luckily he had already decided to leave. He's a cute one. Mine is the only bar he is allowed into in this village.

His walk wasn't the straightest though, and on his way out he bumped right into one of Mad Mary's girls as she came into the pub, carrying her fiddle.

'Hey, watch where you're going,' she said.

'I'll watch when you do,' said Hanly, and took a grip on her upper arm to stop her moving away from him. He wanted a good look at her, now she was so close. Aoife was worth looking at.

With his other hand, grimy and tobacco-stained, he reached up to pull back her hood.

'You have grown into a fine-looking girl,' he said,' his eyes travelling over her face and down her body.

She struggled in his grasp and whispered fiercely: 'Let me go, you old drunk.'

Her nose was wrinkling in disgust at him. I didn't blame

her. The whiskey and the industrial-strength aftershave Hanly uses when he hits the town would tear the lining from the inside of your nostrils.

'Ah, don't be calling me names.'

Hanly peered, a little blearily, into the huge dark eyes that were glaring at him. His grip tightened and he said, his voice wheedling: 'Are you afraid of me? No harm in me, so there isn't. What's yer name?'

The music stopped.

I came out from behind the bar.

'Get away over to your friends now.' I was addressing the girl. Hanly has no friends.

'Leave her now, Hanly,' I said. 'Time for you to be heading home.'

Hanly shrugged and spat on the floor.

'Ah, leave off yourself,' he said. 'I was only looking for a bit of conversation.'

'Yeah, right,' I said.

'You are not half the man your father was. Old James wouldn't have let women take over the pub the way you have.'

'Are you away home?' I asked. 'And are you planning on taking the car?'

'I am,' said Hanly. 'Not that it's any of your fecking business.'

'Well, in fairness, man, I don't think you should be driving. It's a grand clear night and sure you are only a mile or so down the road.'

'It's none of your business how I get home.' Hanly pulled

down his cap. 'You had better get back to your customers.'

He looked like he was going to say more but decided against it. He took a last look over to the alcove where the girl was tuning up her fiddle, her back to him.

'Is that Mad Mary's daughter?'

'It is,' I said. 'She's a grand girl and a great musician but she has her mother's temper. Don't be annoying her, now.'

Hanly jerked his head upwards, spat on the floor and left the bar.

I went over to the girl, who had turned now and was staring after Hanly.

'Now, Aoife, don't go getting any ideas, sure you won't? He will suffer enough when he wakes in the morning, with the head he is bound to have on him.'

She said nothing.

Aoife is a good girl but, as I had said to Hanly, she has a bit of a temper. No wonder, with eejits like Hanly giving her poor mother such a hard time. Mad Mary, they called her. She was just a bit odd in her ways and spent most of her days on the hills. Away with the fairies, like. Aoife is a sharp one though.

I went outside to check on Hanly. His car was still there, the window open and the door not closed properly. Good, I thought, he's decided to walk. I peered down the road. The road to the hills where Hanly lives was overshadowed with flowering hawthorn branches, white like snow and filling the air with the scent of May. The way was lit by bright moonlight. A path to some other world. A path with no one walking on it. Strange he had got out of sight so fast. I shrugged. If he had fallen into a ditch, he could just as well sleep off the whiskey there as in his bed. It was such a beautiful night, I stayed outside for a few minutes, looking at the moon and listening. The call of the old dog fox that haunts those hills came sharply, once, twice, three times. Then nothing. And then what sounded like galloping hooves, far away in the distance.

I turned to go back inside, and I swear to God that old black cat that lives in the barn gave me a grin as wicked as Satan's, licked his paw and then disappeared; business to take care of. We never see much of him on the night of a full moon.

I was woken early the next morning, and pulled myself out of bed, grumpy and bleary eyed. I had been late calling time the night before, the music had been so good nobody had wanted to leave the bar. Someone was trying to start a car outside my window. I looked out – Hanly, come to collect his old banger. In the soft morning air, a single blackbird welcomed the sun. I went down into the yard.

Hanly was revving the car viciously, cursing it.

'Problem with the engine?' I asked.

Hanly growled something and the ignition struck. He began to reverse the car and I laid a hand on the open window, for Hanly was looking terrible. I had seen him looking worse for the wear many times before, but this morning he was bruised and scratched and there were what looked like bites on his face. And I could swear I smelled the bog off him.

'Are you alright?' I asked. 'Did something happen to you

on the way home last night?'

No answer. A growl and a rev so hard the car shot backwards and nearly hit the cat, who was lying in a patch of early sunlight, licking his paw.

Midsummer

On St. John's Eve fires are lighted all over the district and people spend the night singing.

National Folklore Collection

The fairies were very active around Midsummer Eve. During this time, the growth rate continues to increase in pace, coming to the point when it is at its most intense. The earth is warming in the long days. Hillsides become green seas of ferns, ferns that reach and curl into the light of the sun and rise

Midsummer.

to the height of a man. The bright green of early spring has darkened. Spring flowers like the kingcups (marsh marigolds), bluebell and cowslip fade and instead the summer flowers, the foxgloves and honeysuckle, dog roses and poppies begin to bloom.

At the solstice, perhaps our pre-Celtic ancestors walked through fields and woods to the places they had built, making special pilgrimages to sacred sites such as Carrowkeel to see light hit the darkness at the end of a stone tunnel. Midsummer is the hinge. Very, very, slowly the door of light begins to close.

With the peak of growth now over, the time of ripening moves towards the time of harvesting. There is no sense of sorrow in midsummer celebrations, despite the decreasing power of the sun – the hottest part of the summer is yet to come and there is a feeling of being at the zenith of life.

With the arrival of Christianity in Ireland, the summer solstice festivities became tied to 23 June, St John's Eve. The 24 June was celebrated as the birthday of John the Baptist. Even now, bonfires are still lit on hills, a custom that was much more common in times past. Up until the 1950s there were places in the west of Ireland where every hilltop blazed forth in flame. Leaping over the bonfire was one of the common games played at midsummer. Like so many customs, the bonfires, especially the small household ones, had a practical purpose, for they were also a way to clear old rubbish. In many instances, a large bone was placed in the centre of the bonfire, perhaps echoing ritual sacrifice. Sometimes cattle were driven through the embers of the fire. Sometimes charred sticks were brought back to the farms and stuck into the ground to protect the crops or rubbed against the animals to protect the herd. At Knockainey in Limerick, *cliar*, bunches of straw, were lit from the bonfires and brought around the fields, the ashes scattered. Music and dance were an important part of the festivities, as they still are in the celebrations of midsummer in Scandinavia.

In some years the midsummer celebrations coincided with the Feast and Procession of Corpus Christi, which, depending on the date of Easter, could fall as late as 24 June.

But midsummer has very little religious gloss on its festivities. Like Halloween, it was a time when special powers could be gained by collecting the seeds from that fairy plant, the fern. Indeed, if the ritual was celebrated properly the celebrant could rule the world. The fern had to be collected at midnight and a mysterious wind would sweep through the ferns; the devil might even appear. Fern seed could also be used against humans by the fairies, as this tale from the Lough Gur area in County Limerick recounts:

> The 'Good People' would flock around this mortal
> creature. Some of them would throw fern seed in his eyes
> while others would stop his ears with elder pitch so that he
> could not see nor hear. Then little cooks would bring meat
> to him – the meat being that of swallows. The meat tastes
> alright, but as swallows are supposed to have three drops

Foxgloves.

of devil's blood in their veins the meat has a wonderful efficacy on him.

As soon as he eats the meat he is bewitched.

National Folklore Collection

The 23 June was also the day to collect foxgloves, St John's Wort, mugwort and yarrow. Haymaking at midsummer is not connected with any Celtic traditions, as cows in Ireland could usually be pastured outside throughout the winter. The Normans introduced it to Ireland in the twelfth century, so we do not find the straw dolls, goats or crowns that are made at midsummer further north.

THE FIELDMOUSE'S STORY: SÉAN THE PIPER

There is a wealth of folklore associated with Gearóid Iarla, the fourteenth-century lord who was also known as the Wizard Earl and the King of the Norman Fairies. Gearóid was a real person, one of the Norman lords who held positions in the governance of Ireland, who married and had children and was famous for his beautiful poetry, which he wrote in Irish. The Desmond family had integrated totally into Gaelic culture, so much so that the legends surrounding the earl owe a great deal to the older folklore of Lough Gur and Knocfierna, the seat of the sun-goddess, Áine. The earl is sometimes described as being the child of the goddess. He could shape-shift into the form of animals and make himself small enough to fit into a bottle. The prehistoric landscape around Lough Gur is a rich source of legends and folktales, and the place names still hold the echoes of the old stories, stories of Áine of the Black Pig, of the Hag. This particular story begins at the Housekeeper's (aka Áine's) Seat and is a free adaptation of a folktale told by James Butler from the Grange in County Limerick, which is recorded in the National Folklore Collection.

~

Listen carefully, for my voice is very small.

***

Seán Mac Aodha, the great piper, lay sprawled under a hawthorn tree close to the Housekeeper's Seat. He was fast asleep in the sunlight of early evening, around him fields of furze and foxgloves and dog-daisies. Bees hummed and skylarks dipped in the high arch of the sky. Swallows swooped over the still figure. I watched from a safe distance. A mouse can never be too careful when there are humans around.

Seán had been part of a late session the night before, playing at a wake that had gone on close to dawn. It was St John's Eve now, and he had been asked to play later, at one of the bonfires that would be lit on the hillsides in the long light of the June night. He looked as if he could sleep until Doomsday. I crept a little nearer.

Apart from the whiff of poteen, there was a smell of something from him … something delicious. Oatcake. Closer again. The temptation was too much. I slid carefully into his pocket and began to nibble the crumbs. Seán jerked awake.

I whispered: 'Seán, listen, the blackbird has started his evening song. Time to get moving.'

He stood up, and I began to creep from his pocket, hoping he wouldn't put his hand inside and find me there. I had just got my head out when events took a strange turn.

Standing in front of Séan was a tall woman in a green cloak. She was beautiful, her eyes as blue as a midsummer sky, her hair the colour of the sun. She was smiling and throwing a golden ball in the air, then catching it again with a flick of her wrist.

She stopped her game and asked: 'Are you Seán the piper?'

'I am indeed,' he said, blinking stupidly.

'I have come to take you to a great feast,' she said. 'We want you to play music so that we can dance the night away.'

Still fuddled with sleep, Seán shook his head, trying to clear the dregs of last night's fun.

'I thank you my lady, but I have a gig tonight already,' he said.

'We will pay you for more than a hundred gigs.'

The Lady pulled out a green silk purse and opened it.

'Look inside, Seán,' she said. 'See what fills it.'

Seán's eyes lit up. He had never seen so much gold.

'Where is the session, then?' He asked. With a bit of luck, he could fit two sessions in, go on to the one on the hillside later. He could not pass up this opportunity.

'Come with me,' said the Lady, and gestured towards the carriage that was suddenly there in front of us, a black carriage drawn by two of the finest white horses Seán had ever seen, with red-tipped ears and silver shoes. If anything should have warned him that the Lady was of the Sídh it was the red ears on those horses. But Seán, though he was a great piper, was not the brightest shilling in anyone's purse.

He got into the coach and I got in with him. The Lady saw me but said nothing. Mice are friends of the Sídh, also adept at disappearing into the earth when it is necessary. I curled up in Seán's pocket as the horses took off at a furious pace. They went so fast Seán could see nothing beyond a blur of blue and green. The coach stopped with a jolt outside a marvellous crystal castle, where a great crowd of ladies and gentlemen were already feasting and laughing and talking and drinking as if there was no tomorrow.

The Lady offered him wine, and although Seán was seriously tempted to try the hair of the dog, he thought he had better keep his wits about him in this strange company, so he said: 'Not until I have played a few tunes, I thank you.'

He was seated on a chair that glittered with amethysts and crystals and he began to play.

He played 'The Maidrín Rua'. He played 'The Hare in the Corn' and 'The Blackbird and Thrush'. He played 'The Money in Both Pockets' and 'The Maid of the Morning'. He played 'The Hag in the Corner'. He played until his fingers were sore and he felt he might fall over from tiredness, and still he could not stop, and still the great crowd danced.

In despair, he played 'The Tune of Sleeping', but no one fell asleep.

Finally, a dark-haired man with burning eyes came up to him and said, 'Piper, you may stop now, for the dawn is coming.'

And Seán lifted his fingers from his pipes and realised

that there were fishes swimming outside the crystal castle, staring in, open-mouthed, at all the revelry.

'Do you know who I am?' said the man.

And Séan shook in his boots because he knew now he had been taken to the underwater castle of Gearóid Iarla, the Wizard Earl who had disappeared centuries before. Every midsummer dawn he was seen riding over the lake on his white horse with silver shoes.

'Ah, do not be afraid. You will get home safely, for I am no devil, despite the fact that they saw black magic in my bright enchantments. You have already met my mother, fair Áine of Knockainy, and she will bring you back, for I have other things to do.'

'You are really the man who can turn himself into any form of beast or fish or fowl, stag or fox, blackbird or robin or wren?'

The man smiled. 'Oh, the stories they tell about me, half of them the result of drink or sunstroke! That I swam down the Camog in the form of a goose, that I turned myself into a raven and couldn't turn myself back, that I tried to enchant a harmless washerwoman with golden rings … don't believe the half of them, Séan!'

'But will you come back to save Ireland when the silver shoes of your horse wear out?'

'Did no one ever tell you that fairy silver never wears away?'

The Lady Áine came over to Séan and said, 'Time to go home, piper, and here is your payment.'

She handed him the green silk purse, heavy with gold.

The purse went into his pocket, where I lay curled.

'And take a drink now, before you leave.'

Séan drank the red wine put in front of him and fell into a deep sleep.

When he woke up it was midday and the sun was beating down on the slopes of Knockdoon, and he was stretched out between the hawthorn and the furze, exactly where he had fallen asleep the day before. His head felt fuddled, his mouth dry and he could hardly remember what had happened the night before; it came back to him in flashes and starts. He checked first for his pipes; they were safe there beside him. Had it been a dream? Was it still St John's Eve?

I slid out of his pocket just before his hand reached in for the green silk purse. Hiding in the roots of the hawthorn tree, I could see his face drop. Cursing, he threw the purse on the ground.

It was filled with yellow blossom.

The blackbird mocked from the golden furze.

The Booley Girls

For the Irish do not dwell together in an orderly form, but wander with their cattle all summer in the mountains, and all the winter in the woods

A Discourse on the Settlement of the Natives in Ulster, 1628

And now we move into July, the high summertime, which ironically in Ireland was known as the hungry month. Midsummer gives way to the shortages of summer – the last of the stored potatoes eaten, the last cornmeal and grain cooked. Now our forebears waited for the harvest, scraping through, hoping to have enough to keep them alive until the first potatoes could be dug. But even in this hungry time, there were a group of people who probably enjoyed the freedom of summer as much, if not more, than the teenagers of today. These were the young girls who brought the cows to the mountain pastures for the summer booley season.

Ireland and its Cattle

To talk about booleying, we first need to take a look at the cow. We have seen how Irish cows had to be carefully protected on Lá Bealtaine, because for many of our ancestors they were the creatures that stood between a life of relative comfort and a life of want. The lowing of cows resonates through Irish history and culture. Cows are associated with both the winter and summer aspects of the earth goddess. Place names, rivers, towns – many of their meanings are connected to cows and cattle. The Irish language itself owes some basic words to cow, *bó*. The modern Irish word for boy, *buachaill*, has its roots in the word for cowherd while the word for road, *bóthar*, means the way of the cow. The traditional Irish unit of land, the collop, was based not on the size of the plot, but the amount of grazing an animal could get from it.

To give just one example of the ubiquitous nature of cows in early mythology, Fliodhais, the patron goddess of deer and cattle, had a white hornless cow, Maol, who could give enough milk at one milking to feed three hundred men and their families. Her daughters were witches and fairy people, who helped the Tuatha Dé Danann in the Battle of Moytura. Her son had the gift of being able to milk deer for the sustenance of his people. She is a shadowy figure, and there are arguments that she is a medieval invention rather than one of the original gods of the Celts, but her tradition was strong enough for her to be a central figure in one of the cattle-raiding sagas that were the precursors of the *Táin Bó Cuailgne*.

The Cow in Ancient Celtic Lore and Legend

It has been noted that while the *Iliad* has at its centre the abduction of a woman, the great Irish epic tale of the *Táin Bó Cuailgne* has the abduction of a cow. The *Táin* was written down in the twelfth century but dates from much earlier. It is the greatest of the cattle raid poems, poems that constituted a genre in themselves. In defence of our epic, we can claim that the women of the *Táin*, especially the incorrigible Maeve, have a much more active role in the story than they do in Homer's *Iliad*. In the *Táin Bó Cuailgne*, all the trouble starts over the ownership of a bull and it ends with a literal battle between the two bulls at the centre of all the violence, the dark and the white.

The backstory of the *Táin* shows how many forms the bulls took before meeting in their final form. There is a close link between this story and shamanic practices, such as shape-shifting. In Celtic society the cow had a role in such practices, particularly those connected with the selection of a king. In the story of Da Derga's hostel an account is given of the Tarbfeis, where a bull was killed and boiled and a seer had to immerse himself in the cowbath and drink the soup. He then lay down and in his magical trance would identify the most suitable man to be the new king. The druids also built themselves shelters of bull hides stretched on rowan branches, where they would sit and smoke herbs and wait for inspiration. Cows themselves were often magical creatures, appearing from nowhere to give milk to the heroes and heroines of the sagas and the saints of Christianity. Especially powerful were the ones sacred to Manannán, the small white cows with red ears. This breed may have a descendant in the very rare British Chillingforth breed. There are other native breeds still in Ireland, such as the Droimeann, which can range from red to black and which has been saved from extinction by caring breeders. Kerry cows are probably the breed closest to early Irish cattle, which were normally dark coloured or black.

Otherworld beings also sometimes chose to appear to humans as cows. Boann, the river goddess, is closely associated with a white cow. The Great Queen, the Morrigan, appears to Cú as a white cow with red ears, accompanied by fifty heifers, tied together with a chain of white bronze.

The essence of contentment and peace is illustrated by the action of cows lying down in the evening with a sigh – they are remembering the days when the wise king Cormac ruled Ireland. The connections of supernatural acts with cows continued, with saints such as Brighid closely associated with marvellous cows. In folklore, the Glás Gaibhleann provided her owner with an endless supply of milk, until human greed forced her to keep giving until blood came instead of milk, and she turned her back on Ireland.

Cattle in Irish History

Much later, cow-herding was the main occupation of the Elizabethan Irish who lived in the countryside, and cattle raiding was still a feature of Gaelic society in the seventeenth century. The Jacobite Gaelic poets used the lost heifer, the Roisín Dubh – Little Black Rose – as an emblem of Ireland.

Other poems and songs use the image of the lost cow as the symbol of some of the bitterest periods in Irish history. In 'An Druimeann Donn Dílis', the evicted farmer laments the loss of his beloved brown cow. Later again, during the Civil War, in the poem 'The Lost Heifer' Austin Clarke used the straying heifer as a symbol of a vision of Ireland, a vision which had been lost in the bitterness of the bloody conflict. In his descriptions of the riverbank with its 'watery hazes of the hazel', 'brightness drenching through the branches' and 'the mist becoming rain' he also manages to impart the very essence of a misty day in the Irish countryside.

At a much more prosaic level, the Beef Tribunal Report of 1991 is Ireland's most recent cow epic. Transformed into modern legalese almost as impenetrable as the Old Irish of the Táin, it stretches to 580 pages. At the time it was Ireland's longest-running public enquiry, a tale of greed and palm-greasing that exposed a high level of corruption at the heart of our political and financial systems.

In a more humorous, if almost equally appalling way, one of the most popular songs of the Edwardian Percy French celebrated the notion of the woman and cow being part of the marriage bargain. In 'Mc Breen's Heifer', a man is offered a heifer as part of the dowry if he will take the plain daughter instead of the pretty one as his wife. He is left in a quandary:

Oh there's no denying Kitty was remarkably pretty,
Though I can't say the same for Jane,
But still there's not the differ of the price of a heifer
Between the pretty and the plain.

There is some poetic justice meted out to Jamesy Mc Breen; he vacillates between the value of beauty and livestock, and in the end loses both girls.

Apart from their importance in poetry and song, cows were also hugely important in practical terms. Their milk, their flesh, their hides, their fat – used to make tallow for rushlights – every part of them had a use. With its mild winters and long growing seasons, the Irish climate suits cattle raising and milk has been one of the staple foods in Ireland for thousands of years. Bealtaine marked the time when the calving was over, the grass was at maximum growth and the milk yield was at its highest. Although Ireland does not have a strong cheese-making tradition, buttermilk, whey and butter were widely used and valued, with butter especially prized. The Irish sometimes made cakes of cow's blood and butter.

Thomas Smyth's *Information for Ireland 1561* tells us the Irish could get through two thirds of a gallon of butter at a sitting, and the basic diet of the poor in pre-Famine Ireland was potatoes, buttermilk and butter.

In pre-Norman times cows were a basic unit of currency, marking the worth of the owner and used in exchange for other items or as a fee for legal misdemeanours. A milch cow and her calf were highly valued; for the calf was needed to ensure that the cow continued to give milk. Equally important, before milking became a mechanised activity, was the skill of the milker – generally a young girl, who would develop a relationship with the cows and sing to them as she milked. The songs were slow and hypnotic and calmed the cows. Good singers were said to be more likely to be hired as milkmaids, and even after English became the common language spoken in Ireland, milkers would still sing to their charges in the old tongue, claiming it brought more and better milk.

Farming families considered the cows, cattle and horses, as well as the domestic dogs and cats, a part of the household. The National Folklore Collection gives a wonderful array of the names the cows were called, which includes common ones such as Daisy and Strawberry, but also more unusual ones such as The Thieving Cow, Jack Wren and Big Buckley. In Eric Cross's tale of rural life in the 1940s, *The Tailor and Ansty*, Ansty discovers that her heaven cannot really be complete without the presence of her black cow.

Cows are affectionate and placid animals. They respond to kind treatment and are always curious about visitors to their fields, coming over to greet them in their somewhat awkward and comical gallop. Studies of cows have revealed that they play hide-and-seek with each other, have special friends and babysit each other's calves, even at times adopting mother-less newborns without any intervention from humans. While writing this book, I saw cows in a pasture amble over to where a cow and her newborn calf lay dead, and lick them gently as if willing them to get better.

For many centuries it was only the relatively rich farm-ers that owned more than one cow – but to have even one was seen as proof of being secure in the world. Most of the Irish peasantry worked their scraps of land for potatoes, and the livestock was owned by the landlords – at least until the time of the Famine. In the Irish poem 'Bean na dTrí mBó', 'The Woman of Three Cows', (best known in James Clarence

Mangan's English version), the possession of three cows is the reason for the vaunting pride in the woman addressed. There is a correlation between the amount of land owned and the number of cows that could be grazed, but it is a correlation that did not always exist in Irish society. Prior to the land grabs of the sixteenth and seventeenth centuries, in the older Gaelic society, cows were not necessarily kept on land belonging to a specific owner, but grazed freely on the tribal land, moved through the woodlands during the winter months and driven to the upland pastures during the summer. The eighth-century text, the *Senchas Már*, records going out on May Day 'from the green of the old residence to a summer pasture'. Elizabethan Englishmen looked on in amazement at the way the cows were moved to the mountains during summertime, for it was not something done in the southeast of England, where most of the conquerors then came from. In poet Edmund Spenser's opinion keeping cows 'is itself a very idle life and a fit nursery for a thief' – yet another sign of Gaelic fecklessness. He tells us that the Irish 'kept their cattle and lived themselves for the most part of the year in the boolies pasturing on the mountains and wild waste places'.

Cattle rustling was common, and socially acceptable, with the herd driven from place to place to find pasture. Like so much of the native Irish culture, it seemed shiftless and lazy to the English; and the constant movement also made the natives harder to control.

The Booley Girls.

Booleying

The practice of transhumance – moving cattle to different pastures – was known in Ireland as booleying. The name came from the word *buaile*, which originally meant any kind of cattle enclosure. This seasonal movement of the herds was first noted by the Greek writer Phytheas, who recorded the activity among the inhabitants of Thule in the fourth century BCE. It was a widespread aspect of Highland Scottish life, and it is still something that takes place in Scandinavia and Iceland. In the nineteenth and early twentieth century, booleying was based on a simple economic premise – the uplands were used for grazing the cows during the summer months and the grass in the lowland pastures was allowed to grow or was cut for hay. In some cases, as noted by the nineteenth-century travel writers the Halls in Achill, the cows were brought from the inland pastures to the seashore to graze, but it was mainly an activity that took place in the mountainous areas.

Booleying was common all over Ireland, from Wicklow to Tipperary to Mayo. A continuation of the old Gaelic ways, it meant that farmers with little land of their own could manage to feed bigger herds than they would have been able to keep otherwise. But there was more to booleying than economic importance, for the cows stayed in the high pastures for the full summer. The herds needed people to look after them, to milk them and protect them and make butter and cheese to be brought to the home farm. In most cases these were people who could most easily be spared from the work of the farm, so they were sometimes older people, or more commonly, young girls. From Lá Bealtaine onwards these girls went up in groups and lived in the booley houses, very basic stone or sometimes turf huts that had been repaired and made ready for them during April. The houses faced south to make the most of the summer sun, and were sometimes built half underground, thatched with rushes or covered in sods. Sometimes they were located a kilometre or two from each other, and they were usually built in small sheltered valleys with access to a stream.

The simplicity of the life on the hills echoes the hermit's existence. However, booleying was a communal activity, the tasks and the beds were shared, by sisters or friends, unmarried girls whose ages ranged from early teens to early twenties. In some cases younger children came along with the teenagers, and these could include both boys and girls.

These herders sometimes stayed in the summer pastures right up until Samhain, though if they did it must have been a very miserable existence during the last few weeks. There are some reports of them returning to the homestead at Michaelmas (22 September). Their daily routine was simple. They milked the cows, bringing them into the enclosure at night, and spent the day making butter or engaged in such activities as knitting, spinning and sewing. Sometimes the butter was collected but often one or two of the girls would bring it down the mountain to the farmstead. This could be many kilometres away over rough ground – up to thirty kilometres (almost nineteen miles) distant in some cases, though most booley sites were much nearer home. This journey was made about twice a week, and was sometimes the girls' only contact with the rest of the community, although some accounts mention that the booleyers also returned to the valleys to attend Sunday Mass. Within the booley community, small family groups sometimes travelled between the houses, gathering together to sing and dance and exchange news of the world below. Occasionally too, farm lads would travel up to the houses for music and dancing.

There must have been many long wet days on the mountain. The booley houses were very crude, with a hole in the roof rather than a chimney, heather and straw to sleep on and the most basic of furnishings. Imagine trying to get the fire going, or struggling outside to herd the cattle in the icy winds that go ripping down mountainsides, even in May; imagine the mud, the cold, the damp, the dung between the toes. Imagine the potential for bullying and infighting among a group of hormonal teenagers stuck together for many weeks. There is some evidence that there were subtle social controls exercised by the adults on this early form of summer camp, and sometimes an older woman was sent with the girls to keep things under control and possibly instruct them in the tasks that filled the hours between milking and buttermaking. One of the unspoken benefits of booleying may have been the chance to get these disruptive girls away from the community for just a few weeks of the year and also safely away from young men.

But the booley must also have provided a great sense of freedom for these girls; as the scholar Eugene Costello points out in a number of articles, this time provided a liminal space between the restraints of childhood and the new restraints of adulthood. So we can also allow ourselves to imagine how beautiful this world was. Imagine a group of friends laughing in the semi-darkness of the hut when the weather was bad, telling stories to scare each other, teasing, fighting and singing. Imagine being woken up in the morning by birdsong and the lowing of the young cows waiting for you to lead them out onto the mountainside, the grass wet under your feet. The young cows would have been prancing in delight, happy to be out in the fresh pastures. And perhaps there were times when, looking into the blue distances where the land and sky mingle into a haze and become one, brought about a state in these young, giddy creatures which enabled them to see what Scottish writer Nan Shepherd has called the 'mountain behind the mountain', the inner life of the natural world.

Booleying died out in Ireland nearly a hundred years ago, though as late as 1969 there were still people alive who remembered the custom. In some of the accounts of booleying further north, such as Iceland, stories are told of the adventures of the girls who went booleying. Creatures such as shape-shifters, wolves, trolls and the more concrete threat of groups of men could appear through the mountain mist and visit the booley house. There are many variations on the northern European story where the girl climbs a tree and blows a horn for help when such visitors appear. In Ireland, there is a story about a girl who, through a song, warns her little brother, her only companion, that the men who have arrived at the booley mean no good and that he must go to get help, which Little Hugh duly does.

Singing must have been a huge part of the daily lives of the girls on the hills, singing while milking, while churning, while spinning. I spent a long time trying to find out what songs they might have sung in the booley house, songs associated with booleying, with little success. (Scotland seems to have retained a much richer heritage than Ireland in terms of its wealth of working songs). But there are two beautiful songs which celebrate the relationship of a young girl and the cows she looks after. In one of them, the girl laments the fact that she is now married and lives in a town; she curses the people of the town, the glass windows that enclose her, even the priest who married her and mourns the bright mornings, dancing with her '*gamhna geala*', in the quiet of the booley.

The second song, '*Aillilú na Gamhna Geala*' ('Hail, the Bright Calves') is a much more cheerful one, simply the celebration of a summer morning:

> Aililiú the calves, the pretty calves,
> Aililiú the calves, I loved them the best
> Aililiú the calves, the fine pretty calves

Dancing in the meadow on a clear summer's morning
Get me a can and get me a ladle
Get me a vessel to take all the cream
The magic music of the world always around me
But sweeter sounding still the lowing of the cattle to the
parlour

Aililiú na gamhna, na gamhna bána,
Aililiú na gamhna, na gamhna b'iad ab fhearr liom,
Aililiú na gamhna, na gamhna geala bána,
Na gamhna maidin shamhraidh ag damhsa ar na bánta.
Faightear dom canna is faightear dom buarach,
Is faightear dom soitheach ina gcuirfead mo chuid uachtair,
Ceolta sí na cruinne a bheith á síorchur i mo chluasa,
Is gur bhinne liomsa géimneach na mbó ag teacht chun buaile.

The girl and her calves, dancing in the quiet summer mornings; the maybush with its sweet, heady scent, the calling of
the young birds and the plash of forest steams.

Youth and beauty and birds and flowering tree branches – all
bring the summer in.

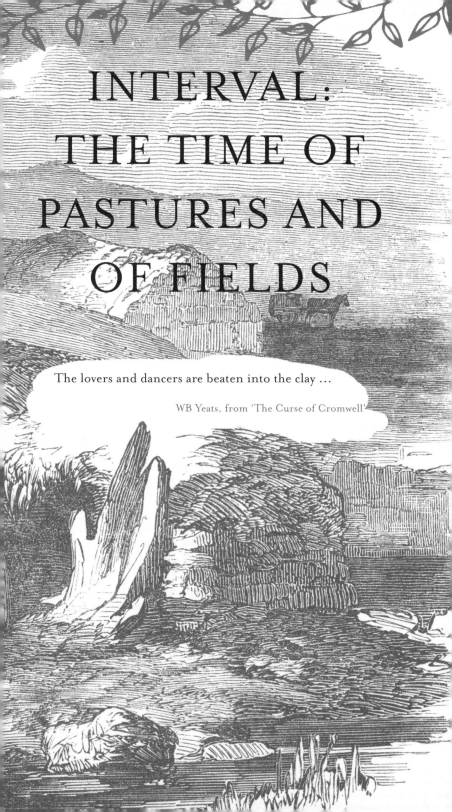

INTERVAL:
THE TIME OF
PASTURES AND
OF FIELDS

The lovers and dancers are beaten into the clay …

WB Yeats, from 'The Curse of Cromwell'

The Field

The time of field and pasture is the shortest reckoning, for it is over in a growing season or a year. But it too marks time, and it is the unit of time that had the most potent and immediate influence on the lives of our forebears. It was vitally important to gauge the size of the year's crop of potatoes, the survival and growth of the herds of cows and sheep, the yield of the cereal crops. When crops failed, people died.

This tie is acknowledged in the Irish language, with, as the writer Manchán Magan points out, its thirty-two words for different kinds of field, and also in the wealth of individual field names:

> The names of the fields are the rushy field, the tuar field, the mountain field, the long field, the small field, the school field, the cross field, the six-acre field, the banshee field, the bog field, the quarry field, … the fort-field, the sports field, the lawn, the step field, gate field, coursing field, the hurling field, the rocky field, the middle field, Coakley's field, the three corner field …
>
> National Folklore Collection

The hayfields and pastures of our ancestors were Elysian places in high summer, containing a wealth of flowers and plants and wildlife now destroyed by us. But it is hard to find beauty in a field of potato drills. The potato does flower, but for most of the year the drills are either ridges of bare brown clay or equally monotonous ridges of withered stalks. Once again, it is what is hidden that counts. The Yukon Golds, the Kerr's Pinks, the Roosters, Earls of Essex, Lumpers, Red Cups, Snowdrops, Green Champions and Golden Wonders are underneath, hidden, sheltered, our old granny potatoes.

Potatoes are our comfort food, in the same way that for the French it is bread, for the Italians pasta. Our annual individual consumption of 85 kilos (187 lbs) of potatoes every year is two and a half times higher than the world average, though it has decreased dramatically from the 140 kilos per annum of the 1990s. Pasta, rice and other more exotic cereals have to some extent replaced the potato as the staple carbohydrate of the main meal of the day. Cereal crops have a relatively short history in Ireland and gluten intolerance continues to be a

Potato diggers.

problem for many Irish people, because of our genetic make-up.

Our comfort food takes many forms; spuds are boiled, mashed, chipped, turned into crisps, mixed into kale for colcannon or flour for potato cakes. Potatoes are celebrated in songs and tunes – the colcannon baked in 'The Little Skillet Pot', the reel called 'The Bag of Potatoes'. In one song, a newly married girl, lonely in her new home, refuses food and drink, and returns at night to her father's house, comforting herself by eating the leftover mashed potato she finds on the dresser. The close identification of the Irish with the potato has given us Spud Murphy, potato faced and any number of racist jokes, many of them told against ourselves. Where but in Ireland would you find Tayto Park, an amusement park called after a brand of crisps?

Yet the potato was only introduced to Ireland in the 1600s, where it soon became a popular crop with the ever-expanding population. Easy to grow, potatoes were planted in what were called lazy beds, a method that was common in Ireland and Scotland but which died out after the Famine. In this method, when planting the tubers in spring, the sod was not removed but turned over. Despite the name, growing potatoes in lazy beds was a physically demanding task, mainly because it was done by humans themselves, not by draught animals. Traces of lazy beds still remain in areas that were depopulated during the nineteenth century, notably Achill Island. Potato growing involved digging, fertilising, building up the ridges, setting the seed potatoes and eventually digging them. But the potato had the huge advantage of being adaptable to poorer soils and a good crop could be grown in even a relatively small area.

Famine

By the mid-nineteenth century, the Irish population of nearly nine million people was largely sustained by small, subdivided plots of potato crops, supplemented by dairy foods such as buttermilk. This is why, when the potato blight arrived in the mid-nineteenth century and destroyed two years' crops in a row, the Irish had no alternative food sources to turn to for survival, for cereal crops were exported from the country, fed to livestock, or sold at a cost that was outside the range of the average cottier. Besides the failure of the potato crops during the consecutive years in 1845 and 1846, there were many other causes of the Great Famine, including government mismanagement, but whatever the causes, the net result was starvation, disease, eviction and emigration, in a pattern that left an indelible mark on the national consciousness. The enchanted landscape had now become cursed; the tiny, rotting potato bodies lay like dead fairies in open tombs, their stench filling the air. The Famine is the great divide. So many were lost to death and emigration; so many more were left in fear, hunger, cold. Evictions followed destitution: many who could not work went to the workhouse to die.

The Famine has also been described as the Great Silencer. The Victorian artist and antiquary George Petrie, travelling through Ireland after the Famine, talks of the silence of desolation. Hooves on the road, the clink of coins, the songs that had been sung and stories told while spinning or herding – these had all been silenced. The hungry grass, that patch of grass which the fairies cursed, so that those walking over it suffered terrible pangs of hunger, became every sod in every potato field.

Known in Irish as *An Droch Aimsire*, the Bad Time, its shadow falls over Ireland well into the twentieth century. The population of over 8 million dropped to 6.5 million in the ten years between 1841 and 1851, and Ireland continued to haemorrhage its healthy young people for a century and a half afterwards. The population of Ireland was at its lowest point of just over four million in 1931 and it is only now increasing to the point that there is more inward than outward migration. The nationalism that flourished in its wake is only one result of the Famine, for its implications for Irish society were far reaching. Such a hugely catastrophic event had major implications for the communal psyche. The Famine deaths were deaths taking place in a country with a mild climate and with good agricultural land. Historians see the power of the Catholic Church as reaching its zenith in the years after the Famine. This was a Church that in Ireland laid huge emphasis on the authority of the priest and the evils inherent in sexual pleasure. The teachings reached fertile ground; to many it must have seemed like a punishment for having so many children, having to watch them all die.

The Great Hunger gives its name to a poem written a century later by Patrick Kavanagh. The poem is in spirit a caoineadh, a great wail of lamentation for the bleak, lonely lives of the small farmers of the 1950s. The spirit of Patrick Maguire, a slave to the misery of working the potato field, any spark of fire or passion crushed by religion and his mother's voice, shrieks at us from a very dark period in Irish rural life.

There is nothing emptier than empty ritual and the poem is filled with rituals and habits that kill all life and light. The famine here is an internal one; it is the poverty, emotional, spiritual, intellectual and sensual, that many small farmers had to endure. These farmers were caught in an impossible bind, for in very many cases a life of marrying and children was denied to them. They might wait until middle age until their father died and they inherited the farm, but if their mother was still alive she had a place in the household until she too died, and there were often problems with the arrival of a new wife into the household. There was also the problem of financial support for a family, which, with any form of birth control apart from abstinence unavailable, could soon become numerous. In 1926 half the men and one third of the women in Ireland were deemed celibate and as late as 1960, the marriage rate in Ireland was the lowest in Europe and the average age of marriage the highest: Irish families, however, were the largest. In 1966, 86% of those people listed in the Never Married category in the census were small farmers or agricultural labourers. While girls frequently also had problems finding husbands, in many cases the young women were leaving the land and heading abroad. What was there to stay for? A place in another woman's house, a baby every year and a lot of very hard work? Many of these girls were only too happy to kick the clay of Meath or Monaghan off their heels and hightail it to England or America, both of which promised a decent life and a freedom unheard of in an Ireland rigidly under the rule of the local parish priest and the religious orders. Even if the only job they could get was as a domestic or on a production line, the money they earned gave them a room of their own and independence, and the chance to meet a mate in a wider environment than the village dance or fair. And so the Patrick Maguires were left behind, in their dun-coloured coats tied with baling string and hands so callused they looked like the potatoes they lifted from the earth:

> Clay is the word and clay is the flesh ...
> We will wait and watch the tragedy to the last curtain,
> Till the last soul passively like a bag of wet clay
> Rolls down the side of the hill, diverted by the angles ...
> The hungry fiend
> Screams the apocalypse of clay
> In every corner of this land.

Patrick Kavanagh, from 'The Great Hunger'

SAVING THE HARVEST IN THE CAHIR MOUNTAINS, KERRY.

Saving the Harvest.

LUGHNASA

Those merry couples

dancing in tune

WB Yeats from
'The Wanderings of Oisin'

FAIRS, FESTIVALS AND HARVEST

The corn was orient and immortal wheat, which never
should be reaped, nor was ever sown. I thought it had
stood from everlasting to everlasting.

From 'Centuries of Meditation' by the English poet
and mystic Thomas Traherne (1637–1674)

Lughnasa is named for Lugh, the stranger god who
joined the Tuatha Dé Danaan in the battle against his grandfather, Balor. This is the bright one, the many skilled, whose
cloak has the red glow of the sun at evening, and who gave
his name to the festival that celebrates the harvest and the
period from the beginning of August to the end of October.
This is the god who established the great fair or gathering at
Tailteann at harvest time. The connection of the beginning of
Lughnasa and these celebrations means that unlike the other
festivals, Lughnasa is not tied to a specific date or days, but
rather covers the period from towards the end of July into the
first weeks of August.

The Tailteann fair began as Tailtiu's funeral games, a commemoration of the foster mother of Lugh who died from
exhaustion after she had cleared the great plain in the centre
of Ireland. The forests and underbrush gone, the ferns and the
brambles razed, the people could now grow and harvest crops.
Harvest, sovereignty, assembly, sport and social and commercial gatherings – these are the keynotes of the Lughnasa
season, in traditions that have lasted until the present day,

though the form they take has changed. Nowadays August in Ireland is marked by the celebrations of festivals and games, notably the GAA hurling championships, with the national final held between late August and early September.

THE KING'S STORY: HOW SETANTA WAS NAMED

This is a story about hurling, one of Ireland's national sports, and its most ancient. It tells the tale of the first of the great deeds of the hero Cú Chulainn, so of course it involves a death. Cú Chulainn was the greatest of Irish warriors, famous for his battle fury, when his bones turned backwards, his mouth twisted until it met his ears and one eye sunk into his head while the other protruded outwards. Fire and blood shot from his body and skull. This story predates these impressive performances but it does give us the sense of a child who knows very well how to look after himself, something that was obviously necessary with a 'forgetful' uncle like Conchubar. I have always wondered how it could slip the mind of Setanta's uncle that his nephew was on his way to Culann's house. Conchubar Mac Nessa is one of the less attractive of the ancient kings, not least because of his pursuit and murder of the sons of Usna and his treatment of Deirdre thereafter.

~

I am the king. Be still and listen to my story.

The Old Hooded One said to me that the best-laid plans of men can sometimes go astray. She was to be proved right. But it was not so much a plan, as an impulse. I am the king and when I have an itch, I scratch it. What happened that day was a response to an annoying young boy who seemed to know too much, who was a little too proud of his own prowess. Did I really want Setanta dead? I don't know. It was as well he lived, for he defended the North when no other warrior could be roused from sickness. And yet …

***

It was late summer, a fine day, a day when every lad in the court was out practising with his weapons or playing ball on the green of Emhain Macha. As for me, myself and my retinue had been invited to a feast at the house of the smith Culann, and we set off in mid-morning, for it was a long journey. I was in a bad mood to start, as I knew I was in for a boring evening. Culann can spend hours boasting about his fast steeds, his fertile herds, his savage hounds. But you never refuse an invitation to a feast, unless you want to make an enemy for life. It is the insult of insults. And Culann is a useful man, the greatest of smiths. He would make a dangerous enemy.

We passed the green where the young ones were playing hurling, and I stopped a moment, for there in the middle was my sister's child, Setanta. His mother, lovely Deichtine, was dead now. She died of grief soon after the birth, when the shame of the child was on her. I regret that. But I don't regret what happened that night, the night we found ourselves stranded in the snow after a wild chase of magic birds. All of us drinking. Afterwards, I made sure that a rumour spread that the god Lugh was the child's father. There was no need for her to take the whole affair so badly.

I thought of her as I stood and watched the beautiful arc

of hurley and sliotar as my nephew raced towards the goal, enjoying the melee that is a hurling game, the running and the pulling and the shouting. I soon realised that there was something odd about this game. It seemed as if all the boys were ranged against Setanta, who was defending his own goal and attacking the other goal at the same time. It seemed he was a team of one. And that team of one was winning. No other child could take control of the ball.

I called out, and the boys stopped playing and came over to me, Setanta bringing up the rear, as if reluctant to pause the play. Setanta – small, dark and a bit ill-favoured.

I stared at him and he stared back at me. That child had the strangest eyes.

'You do well, child of my sister,' I said to him.

He inclined his head as if the praise was his due.

'Come with me to the house of Culann the Smith as a prize for your skilful play.'

The boy shook his head. 'The game is not finished here.'

'That's alright,' said one of the other boys. 'You might as well go now. We have lost count of the number of points you have scored.'

'Yeah,' said another. 'We'll manage without you.'

Once more the child shook his head.

'I will follow on,' said Setanta. 'I will finish here first.'

I shrugged. Did this young pup expect me to wait for him?

'Come then, when you are finished here,' I said. 'We need to be on our way.'

At Culann's house, the smith, a short man with wrestler's

arms, welcomed us in, to where a huge feast was spread out on the tables. Musicians and poets and vats of drink. All that might be expected to welcome the king.

The sun had started to go down, and Culann asked if he should loose his guard dog to keep us safe and secure within the walls.

'For if news gets out that you are here, King Conchobar, your enemies may come to attack you.'

I nodded. We went outside to where the huge black beast was chained with seven chains. He was a devil dog, snarling and howling at us as we approached. Culann took an iron bar and held it high as he went to undo the chains.

'Get back inside as soon as I start to loose the chains,' he said. 'This dog will eat anyone that is outside. I am the only one that can control him, and that is because he knows the weight of my arm.'

We went in, and feasted.

The sun set and the feast grew rowdier. The moon rose, hardly more than a crescent as it approached its last quarter.

I swear to you, it was only when I heard the rumpus outside, the growling and the howling, the barking and the choking, that the memory of the child Setanta came into my head.

Well, I thought – that's the end of the gifted child.

But then there was a single savage howl. Culainn took up his iron bar and we rushed outside. Lying in the moonlight was not the mangled remains of a child but Culann's great hound, stretched dead on the grass, its jaws opened wide and a sliotar lodged in its throat.

The child looked unperturbed.

'It jumped right at me,' he said. 'I let loose with my hurley. I had to kill it.'

I could find nothing to say. This child was more than a prodigy. This child had the protection of the gods. Perhaps Lugh was his father after all.

Then Culann said, 'That is all very well, but where will I get another such dog to guard my house?'

Culann, a cruel man with an iron bar and a short temper.

Opportunities arise and one takes them. I looked into Setanta's eyes and I saw madness there, and grief to all that came close to him.

'Setanta,' I said. 'You have killed this man's guard dog. I charge you with guarding his house until another such hound can be raised. You will stay here for seven years; you will not leave off the guarding until then, you will not leave this house. And to mark this event, I will give you a new name, henceforth you will be called the Hound Of Culann.'

And so Cú Chulainn got his name.

The Festival of Lughnasa

We do not know the date of the origin of the great Assembly and games which celebrated Lugh and his foster mother. But the presence of huge prehistoric earthworks at Tailtiu in County Meath, modern Teltown, indicate that ritual events on a large scale were held here long before the sixth century, when the written records of the Lughnasa assembly begin.

These records tell us that it was an obligation of the High King at Tara to hold at least one such great Assembly, the Óenach Tailteann, during his reign. This great fair or assembly survived in various forms until the coming of the Normans. In 1168 the Annals record that the lines of horses and vehicles travelling to the Assembly stretched to six miles. The tradition of a fair at Lughnasa survived for centuries. A much smaller, local event was held at Teltown until 1770. By this stage the fair had fallen into disrepute because of drunkenness and violence. Drinking and fighting seem to have been a feature of Irish fairs throughout modern times. The infamous Donnybrook Fair even gave its name to a slang term for a brawl, though fighting is not mentioned in the eighteenth-century ballad, 'The Humours of Donnybrook'. It does, however, give a vivid picture of the fair:

Donnybrook Fair.

There horsemen and walkers and likewise fruit-hawkers
And swindlers the devil himself that would dare
With pipers and fiddlers and dandlers and diddlers
All met in the humours of Donnybrook Fair
'Tis there are dogs dancing and wild beasts a-prancing
With neat bits of painting, red, yellow and gold
Toss players and scramblers and showmen and gamblers
Pick-pockets in plenty, the young and the old
There are brewers and bakers and jolly shoemakers
With butchers and porters and men that cut hair
There are montebanks grinning, while others are sinning
To keep up the humours of Donnybrook Fair.

In some cases the violence was contained within the social framework of wrestling bouts and the fairtime bouts may have performed the function of providing a safety valve for violence in the community. Other functions of fairs included trading livestock, hiring servants, hearing the latest ballads and purchasing household goods. As late as the 1930s, the fairs and markets were very important parts of rural life, indeed an essential form of social cohesion in a society whose members had few opportunities for locals to meet people outside their neighbourhood. The children who contributed to the Folklore Survey were able to ream off the names of local fairs, many of them specifically for the sale of different farm animals. But by the 1930s the fairs were beginning to die out. Custom-built marts replaced the fairground or market square, no doubt improving public hygiene, for hundreds of animals gathering in the centre of a town and blocking the traffic must have been a very messy and smelly occasion. In 2020, due to Covid restrictions, the first virtual mart was held.

At the Óenach Tailteann violence was forbidden. Nor is there any mention of dancing, an activity which became an integral part of later fairs. But despite these limitations, the Óenach Tailteann was the fair to go to, whether it was to trade horses, link up with friends and allies, bet on the races or find a wife. The Assembly was also where you went to find out what your political leaders had decided for your future. Laws were made at the Assembly and announced to those gathered there. Matches were made between couples, which were different from those made in other settings. The Teltown Marriage tradition was an early form of divorce, where a couple who decided that they were not suited could go through a cere-mony of separation at a certain date after their wedding. Originally the day of the possible split was Bealtaine, but later this changed and a year and a day became the length of time the couple were given to decide whether or not to continue as partners. Custom has it that they walked away from each other, one to the north and one to the south, out of the fort at Teltown if they wished to end the marriage. Interestingly, in folk tradition, the received wisdom was that August was not a good month to get married in.

The God Lugh

Lugh, the god credited with founding the Tailteann gathering, is a latecomer to Ireland, arriving around the first century. He was a pan-Celtic god, worshipped in continental Europe and giving his name to Lyon and Carlisle. He has many of the attributes of a solar god, though as the Many-Skilled, he was also identified by Roman writers as akin to Mercury, introducing us to the civilised activities of bargaining and diplomacy. In his identification with games and play Lugh also resembles Mercury, as he is said to have introduced Fidchell (a board game similar to chess), ball-playing and racing to Ireland. Highly skilled in every craft, he has sometimes been linked to the Gobán Saor, the folk hero and master craftsman who is supposed to be buried at Derrynaflan Church in Tipperary, the site of the Derrynaflan Hoard, which contains some of the most beautiful gold work found in Ireland. The gold of Lugh's harvest and his cleverness is also linked to that master shoemaker, the Leprechaun, with his pot of gold and ability to trick his captors.

In the sagas, Lugh's skills are such that he is a major player in the epic battle of Moytura, siding with the Tuatha Dé Danaan against the Fomorians, led by Balor of the Evil Eye, his grandfather. At this battle he is the one who kills Balor, the monster whose single eye could flash out and kill like a bolt of lightning. The lack of family affection on Lugh's part can be explained by the fact that Balor wanted to kill his grandson at birth, but was thwarted by the woman of the Sídh who carried him over the sea from Tory Island to the safe arms of Tailtiu, his foster mother. After the Dé Danaan victory in the battle, Lugh shows his powers of diplomacy. As we have seen, rather than killing his enemy Bres, he makes a deal with the Fomorian leader. If Bres shares his knowledge of ploughing and sowing and reaping the harvest, his life will be spared. With Lugh, we are at the beginning of the temporal move from the mythical and megalithic into the realm of history; of kings and kingship, of contracts and oaths sworn and battles fought not for cattle but for lordship.

Harvest Time: Patrick and Lugh

How did the festival of Lugh survive right into the twenty-first century, for the god himself, is, despite his brightness, a shadowy figure? The secret perhaps lies in the time of year and the ripening of the harvest, and the festivities that were celebrated long before the worship of Lugh began in Ireland. The survival of the Lughnasa traditions so wonderfully recorded in Máire Mac Neill's book, *The Festival of Lughnasa*, has as much to do with the simple desire of people to gather together, to celebrate the arrival of harvest time as it has with the celebration of any god. After the introduction of the potato to Ireland, the end of July and the beginning of August became even more important to the country people of Ireland. In addition to the beginning of the grain harvest, the 'earlies' of the potato crop, which had become a staple food of the poor in Ireland by the eighteenth century, could now be harvested. So at this time there were a number of reasons to celebrate. Food was plentiful again. The days were often warm and sunny. What other excuse was needed for young people to climb into the hills and meet with each other, to dance in the summer sunset and gather bilberries? As we are in Ireland there will always need to be another reason, and in nine cases out of ten that reason will be religion.

For Lughnasa is an extreme example of a pagan festivity that was culturally appropriated by Christianity. And it has our national saint, our Bishop Patrick, there at the core of it. For according to tradition, on the summit of Croagh Patrick, a mountain that was one of Ireland's high holy places from long before the saint's time, Patrick wrestled with demons and fought, not just for his own soul but for the soul of Ireland itself. Dark demons assaulted the saint but he held firm and was succoured by white-winged birds, angels of light. Patrick gained special privileges for the Irish, and his victory is commemorated every Reek Sunday, which is either held on the last Sunday in July or the first Sunday in August – at Lughnasa. The complicated ritual of the day includes rounding, a practice that involves circling the various structures on top of the hill, including its three cairns. Although there is a pathway up the mountain, it is no easy climb, but despite this and the weather conditions, which are often atrocious, thousands take part in the annual pilgrimage. In 2019, it was estimated that 2000 people climbed the Reek, some of them barefoot, despite being advised to avoid the climb because of storm conditions.

At Lughnasa, Patrick is also celebrated as the one who defeats Dark Croucher, Crom Dubh, who is merged with another creature of darkness, Crom Cruach. This evil creature crawls out of the dark pagan past into the light of the new religion. Crom demanded tributes of milk, of the harvest and of children from the people of Ireland. He was the Evil One, the devil (or 'idol' worshipped by the pagans) defeated by Patrick. In one poem Patrick is described as taking a sledgehammer to the stone idol Crom Cruach.

The Croagh Patrick Pilgrimage.

Folklorist Dáithí Ó hÓgáin sees it as likely that Crom and Patrick replaced Balor and Lugh as the Lughnasa battle opponents. In another version of Crom Dubh's defeat he is buried under the earth by St Brendan, with his head exposed so that the saint could baptise him. Once again there is the connection with harvest and corn. St Brendan literally waters Crom Dubh, his head coming forth from the earth like a blade of wheat.

The nineteenth-century Irish poet and antiquary Samuel Ferguson gives an interesting account of how such a transfer from pagan to Christian could happen as late as the mid-nineteenth century; his correspondent, Mr O'Looney, tells the story of how the festivities held at the 'Sun Altar' at

Mount Callan in County Clare on the first of August, Crom Dubh's Sunday, were deliberately replaced by the local priest with a pattern (devotions that occur on the feast day of a patron saint) to the nearby St Munchan's Well. Many of the numerous patterns held in late July and early August, some of them still celebrated by large numbers of people, had their origins in Lughnasa celebrations.

Music, Dance and Water

The Christian pilgrimage has survived longer than the other more universal elements of the Lughnasa tradition. By the 1930s the trips to the top of local hills to gather bilberries, as recorded by Máire Mac Neill, were becoming a memory.

The pre-Christian festival seems to have lacked strict rituals, or at least any that survived. Bilberries were picked and were eaten or made into crowns or bracelets by young girls and young men. Lughnasa was very much a young person's festival and it was a relaxed one. The hillside sites were difficult for older people to get to, so young people could be sure of being left to themselves.

For the girls booleying on the mountains it must have provided a welcome break from the loneliness and boredom of being isolated with their own small group of companions. (It may even be possible that there was a connection between the presence of the booley girls in the hills and the survival of the festival, as both booleying and the Lughnasa festival declined at around the same time.)

There was singing and music and dancing – the dancing

celebrated in Brian Friel's play, *Dancing at Lughnasa*; music and dance create their own communities, pulling people together into shared experience in a way few other activities can. Traditional music and dance are still celebrated today in the more formal and competitive atmosphere of the annual Fleadh Cheoil, normally held in August, and much less formally in the regular traditional music and dance sessions held in pubs and in the summer music festivals. There was music and sun and freedom; this was when summer romances began, romances which might not outlive the harvest. As one saying put it, a bundle tied in August would be ripped in September.

The Lughnasa festival was one where fire does not seem to have held the significance it had at the times of the other great feasts. Though there are some accounts of bonfires, water

Dancing by water.

seems to have held greater significance. Again, this is a natural response to the season. Every summer, humans flock to
the sea, to lakes, to places where we can immerse ourselves,
escape the heat – if we are lucky enough to have any – and
also to create a space where we give ourselves permission to
play. While there was still work to be done – lambs were sep-
arated from their mothers at this period, ending the cycle that
began at Imbolg – the main bulk of the harvest work would
not begin until later in August and into September. Therefore,
there was more time for races and ball-playing, Lugh's gifts to
the Tuatha Dé Danaan.

Water played an important part in the July and August
games that marked this holiday season. In places where there
were no hills to visit, trips were made to lakes, to rivers and
to holy wells. There was an ancient element of purification in
driving animals such as cows and horses through water, but
there must also have been the simple pleasure of the fun of the
thing. In 1818, on the second Sunday in August, we are given
an account of horse swimming in Lough Owel. Could this
be a continuation of a ritual of bathing horses that stretches
back to the days of the kings? The horses were immersed with
riders on their backs, and swimming races were held in the
water, an exercise that was dangerous and sometimes fatal.
Priests discouraged such activities, not least because the boy
riders sometimes rode naked. According to the pre-Famine
Ordnance Survey Letters, during the Lughnasa celebrations,
spancels and halters were thrown into the lough at Bohola
in Mayo as an offering, an activity with strong echoes of the
prehistoric bog offerings.

The Plough and the Horse

The fort over against the oak-wood,
Once it was Bruidge's, it was Cathal's,
It was Aed's, it was Ailill's,
It was Conaing's, it was Cuiline's,
And it was Maelduin's;
The fort remains after each in his turn—
And the kings asleep in the ground.

'The Fort at Rathangan', translation by Kuno Meyer

The almost primal connection with the horse is seen in a wide range of aspects of Irish life. Some are enshrined in our politics and some are more organic. Political attempts to revive a tradition that has reincarnated itself into other forms are likely to fail; one example of which is the abortive attempt made by the Irish government to reinstitute the Tailteann

Games in 1924. This attempt had died a death by the 1930s as the effort made to get young people interested in the ancient ways and games lacked glamour. The most successful event by far was the motorcycle race. The closest successor to the ancient Tailteann games is not this failed endeavour but the National Ploughing Championships, held every year in September. This initiative sprang directly from the Irish people themselves. It started in local inter-county ploughing competitions, which were given a broader structure in the 1930s. The year 2020 was the first time since their foundation that the Championships were not held. In its emphasis on skill, on commerce and on merrymaking, it is the direct descendant of the ancient gatherings.

The horse plough came to Ireland at the same time as the Normans, and for nine centuries, until wide-scale mechanisation was introduced in the late 1930s and 1940s, the ploughman was an integral part of the rural landscape during spring and autumn.

The Ploughing Championships are held in September, at a time when there is a natural gap in the farming year – apart from maize the tillage crops have all been gathered in. The National Ploughing Championships started off as a voluntary effort, with only nine counties competing when it was first held in 1931. Since then its growth has been phenomenal. The Championships are now held over a three-day period and in 2019 nearly 300,000 visitors attended. The festival was born during dark years, the years of struggle following national independence. Tillage had declined as a farming activity, but there was a strong drive towards making Ireland self-sufficient in terms of its foodstuffs. 'One more sow, one more cow, one more acre under the plough' as the Minister for Agriculture, Paddy Hogan, succinctly put it. The major aim of the Championships was to encourage excellence in the art of ploughing, but it also aimed to provide 'a pleasant and friendly place to do business'. This statement has the ring of the ancient *aonach* (fair) and at the same time demonstrates the hard-headed business element of the Championships. Both of these elements had a part to play in the success of the venture. But the organisational skill of those who run the event was also a major key to its success.

The site of the championships is in a different location every year, thus making it extremely inclusive and bringing business to all parts of the country. In 1933 the championships were held in Clondalkin, now a sprawling suburb of Dublin, and as late as 1971 it was held in Finglas, another Dublin suburb. I had the privilege of listening to some Laois farmers discuss their route to the 2019 championships, and I had the feeling of being drawn into an ancient world of gatherings, of fairs and assemblies, with the chariot routes from all over Ireland carefully delineated, all leading, like the spokes of a wheel, to the axle of the assembly. People from each county have to take a specific route and are guided to their section of the 800-acre complex. It's a wonder of logistics, and despite the large commercial element it is still mainly organised by volunteers. The exhibitions and competitions now include much more than just ploughing, but cover all aspects of rural life. There is a very popular brown bread baking competition. Ballads have been written about the Championship, and in an effort to encourage female participation, in 1950 the Farmerette Class (it is no longer called this) was introduced. A few years later an extra incentive was given to the Farmerettes – if the winner was under twenty-five and got married during the year after the championships she would receive £100 on her wedding morning. This looks like a deliberate tactic to keep girls on the land, a response to the mass exodus of young women from the countryside at this time.

There is still a horse ploughing category in the Ploughing Championships and the horse is also at the centre of some of the major social events in the Irish calendar, not just in summer but all the year round. Hundreds of races are held throughout the year in Ireland, point-to-point races, National Hunt and hurdle races, all with a strong social element to them, a focus for community bonding. During Lughnasa there is an intensification of this equine activity, from the Dublin Horse Show to the strand races held all over the country, from Laytown in Meath to Lacken in Mayo. One of the main functions of the original assembly at Tailteann was that the king should be seen by his supporters and presented with tributes

by them, and this inevitably raises the image of the infamous Ballybrit Racecourse tent. During the late twentieth and early twenty-first century, the leader of the Fianna Fáil party held court at Ballybrit in Galway, where donations were received from all and sundry, including property developers. The 'tent' was cancelled in 2008, mainly because of the controversy surrounding donations. The link between the power of the sovereign and the Lughnasa races goes deep.

Mythical Horses and the Cult of the Leader

The cult of the horse in Ireland goes deeper even than political power. Horse bones are found buried in Newgrange and the primal image of the horse, particularly the white horse, is buried deeply in our collective psyche. Delight in horse racing goes very far back; it was an important amusement in the pre-Christian otherworld. Our equine friend appears in folklore as the scraggy grey horse of the Gille Deacair, as the magical púca who takes unsuspecting humans on crazy night rides; as the water horses which rise suddenly out of lakes. The Sídh are often recorded as passing in a whirlwind of racing steeds, sometimes using ragwort as their mounts. The king Labraidh Loinseach even develops the features of a horse – its ears – and in the tale of Donkeyskin the princess disguises herself under a donkey skin to escape the incestuous advances of her father. Horses are also hugely important in the sagas, both Christian and pre-Christian. They are loyal companions to heroes such as Cú Chulainn and saints such as Colmcille, weeping at the death of their owner. We have seen how horses and their paraphernalia were sacrificed to the gods in the bogs and the infamous horse bath ritual recorded by Giraldus Cambrensis in the twelfth century, long derided as a slur on the Gaelic kings, may have its roots in a ritual mating of the lord of the land and the sovereign horse goddess, the goddess of the land and fertility. It is worth quoting in full:

> There is in the northern and farther part of Ulster, namely Kenelcunill [Tyrconnell], a certain people which is accustomed to consecrate its king with a rite altogether outlandish and abominable. When the whole people of that land has been gathered together in one place, a white mare is brought forward into the middle of the assembly. He who is to be inaugurated, not as chief, but as a beast, not as a king, but as an outlaw, embraces the animal before all, professing himself to be a beast also. The mare is then killed immediately, cut up in pieces, and boiled in water. A bath is prepared for the man afterwards in the same water. He sits in the bath surrounded by all his people, and all, he and they, eat of the meat of the mare which is brought to them. He quaffs and drinks of the broth in which he is bathed, not in any cup, or using his hand, but just dipping his mouth into it round about him. When this unrighteous rite has been carried out, his kingship and dominion has been conferred.

We find so many white horses in the legends and tales: the horse goddess Macha; Gearóid Iarla, who circles Lough Gur on a white steed; and Oisín, who travels to the land of the young on Niamh's great white horse, and comes back to find that the old order has disappeared and a new one has taken its place. We have yet another white horse marking the arrival of a new sovereign: the white mare of King William of Orange.

The Twelfth of July

King William is most often portrayed in folk art of murals and banners as crossing the Boyne, the river that flows between two of the ancient Irish kingdoms. William rides triumphant, his sword raised in challenge, proclaiming victory for a new political and religious regime. This is the quintessential symbol of the defeat of the Gaelic and Catholic powers of Ireland. It celebrates the defeat of the forces led by King James by William of Orange, and is still marked every twelfth of July. The festival originated in the amalgamation of the smaller celebrations of two July battles, that of Aughrim (1691) and that of the Boyne (1690), but for reasons perhaps not unconnected with folk memory and more specifically the presence of a king on a white horse and a royal river, it is the Boyne battle that is celebrated, just at the hinge of the Lughnasa period. The Twelfth of July marches took their present form after the establishment of the Orange Order in 1795. The first marches were in 1796, and they have continued ever since, becoming in some cases a political flashpoint for conflict between Nationalist and Unionist communities. The marches also signal the lighting of victory bonfires, and both were sometimes marked by violent disorder, so much so that some of them were banned during the nineteenth century.

On the Twelfth, the marchers move slowly along, playing music or carrying local banners, often accompanied by children running alongside the pipers and drummers. There are elements to the marches that give them an anachronistic feel – the young men wearing the sashes and bowler hats of a bygone age, the middle-aged ladies dressed in Union Jack outfits. The colour orange figures prominently, as do children with their hair dyed blue and red. And then there is the Lambeg drum. The drum shares with the bagpipes the honour of being the loudest acoustic instrument in the world. The drum calls the tribe together and cannot be ignored. The bigger and louder the march, the more likely it is to spark a response of rage. Yet, if we are to look at this island as an entity, it is just as much a part of Irish identity as a St Patrick's Day Parade, some might argue even more so, as it more clearly reflects a native tradition, where as much of St Patrick's Day is imported from second- and third- and sixth-generation Irish. On a more local level, the Derry Apprentice Boys Parade, traditionally held in August, contained the same element of defiance and tribal bombast, though in recent years attempts have been made to transform it into a less politicised and more inclusive festival.

Lughnasa Sports

The tribal divisions of the island of Ireland are also still an undercurrent in that other inheritance from Lugh, hurling. Hurling is mentioned in the earliest sagas and was a very popular sport throughout the centuries. The eighteenth century was especially notable for its community matches between different villages or big landed estates. In early nineteenthcentury Ireland, on May Day, hurling balls decorated with gold and silver cloth were presented by newly married couples to the young men of the district. The struggle for possession of these May balls often ended in violence and the custom was encouraged to die out. Gaelic football also has a long ancestry, but the revival of both sports in the nineteenth century was a very political act. The Gaelic Athletic Association was founded in 1876 as an integral part of the Irish Nationalist movement, and many revolutionary figures were prominent in its ranks. This identification of the GAA with Nationalism has lasted ever since. A ban on those employed in the British security forces from joining the GAA lasted until 2001. The second infamous ban, that on playing foreign games or even dancing foreign dances, was removed in 1971, not before Douglas Hyde, the first president of the Irish Republic and one of the great scholars and promoters of Irish culture, was removed as a patron of the GAA because he attended a soccer match between Poland and Ireland in 1938. Competition, creating a sense of unity against a rival is probably the fastest way to create the sense of belonging, a sense of being part of a community, but it is a double-edged sword because it needs the 'other' to exist in order for it to exist itself.

The Lughnasa season sees the culmination of the GAA season, the National Finals in Gaelic football and hurling, held at the end of August and early September. These matches are played by amateur players and the teams are strictly tied to their counties. Indeed, it has been said that there was no real sense of county loyalty in Ireland before the GAA. Here identification with a team and the sense of community and excitement among players and supporters reaches its zenith and takes on an almost religious fervour. Hurling, played with a hurley and ball, is a game of considerable skill, intensity and speed and it can become very heated on occasions, with a lot of jersey pulling and shoulder-to-shoulder charges. During the 1990s I had the embarrassing experience of telling some French friends, new to Ireland, to have a look at the hurling match being shown on TV. I hoped that they would be impressed by the players' skill and the vertiginous speed of the game; and also that they wouldn't ask me about the rules, as I had no idea what they were. 'Our national game!' I said proudly. As we looked on, the field erupted into a very physical free-for-all between the two teams. This was the first and last time I have seen such a thing happen: the timing was impeccable.

Fairies and ghosts have been known to play both football and hurling, and one Holy Lake was formed by a group of hurlers who asked a passing woman if there were any wells in

the vicinity, as the game had made them thirsty. She told them to pull a rush, but be sure to replace it when they were finished drinking from the well that would appear. They forgot to do so and they were drowned, but their ghosts can be seen rising from the lake on the anniversary of their disappearance, still playing their ghostly hurling match.

Puck Fair

Before we leave the sunlit heights of Lughnasa and move towards the end of the harvest and the equinox, it is worth emphasising once again the importance of fairs to rural communities. As we have seen, they were a break from the endless monotony of hard physical labour, a place to dance and listen to music, to meet a mate, to buy novelties unseen the rest of the year, and, most particularly if you were a man, to get very drunk.

Puck Fair, Killorglin, 1880.

Some fairs were large annual events, with people coming from long distances. A number of larger towns held Christmas fairs, but the Lughnasa period saw dozens of different fairs all over the country. People travelled for miles to attend the Ballycastle Lammas Fair, some of them coming by boat from Islay in Scotland. At the other end of the country we have the most famous of Irish fairs, the horse and cattle fair traditionally held in mid-August in Killorglin, County Kerry.

Puck Fair's origins are lost in folklore, though some scholars claim that it is unlikely to have existed before the later Middle Ages. The reason most often given for the Puck (the male goat) becoming the symbol of the fair is that in the Middle Ages, most fairs were given a mascot, usually an animal. But why the Puck, and why the strange ceremonies that are part of the fair? A Puck or poc, traditionally a 'wild mountain goat' (though these are thin on the ground these days) is set on a stand high above the fair and crowned King Puck by the Queen of Puck, a local schoolgirl. On the third day of the fair the goat is released back into its home in the mountains.

The first record of a fair in Killorglin is in 1613, some decades before the date of one of the main legends of the fair's origins. It is said that when Cromwellian soldiers were on their way to attack the town, a wild mountain goat came down from the hills and warned the inhabitants of the danger, and the fair was established in his honour.

Whatever its origins, Puck Fair was traditionally a wild affair, reflecting the untamed and independent nature of its patron animal. Goats are hardy creatures, able to graze in mountainous areas unsuitable for cattle or even sheep. There are still numbers of wild goats in Ireland, and domestic goats have the virtue of giving good milk, but they have never been farmed to any intensive degree.

In Ireland, goats do not have the strong association with the devil and witches that they have in England, though the cloven hoof is very much a sign of the Prince of Darkness and the Púca could sometimes take the form of a goat. Perhaps one reason for the connection between the fair and the goat was the fact that goats were symbols of fertility and virility and therefore by default linked to the time of year when children were often conceived. The juxtaposition of a young girl – at around twelve years of age the Queen is on the cusp of puberty – and the Puck as King is telling and in some ways slightly unsavoury.

In recent years there have also been concerns expressed for the welfare of an animal exposed to the crowds and noise of the fair for three days, but there is no sign of the tradition of King Puck being discontinued. However, attempts have been made to take the feral edge off Puck Fair by making it a more family friendly affair.

In times past, country people came down from the hills and Travellers from all over Ireland arrived in droves, for the fair was always very much connected with the Travelling Community. In RTÉ archive footage from 1967 there is a report on the efforts of the local council to push the Travellers' caravans back from the centre of the town, in an early effort at gentrification.

Puck Fair is not for the faint-hearted. The American poet Muriel Rukeyser wrote a book about visiting it in the 1960s, revealingly entitled *The Orgy*, and much of her time seems to have been spent avoiding drunks and picking her way through piles of manure and pools of vomit. This edginess, and the element of drunken wildness, has not gone away despite the introduction of international elements such as BBQ kangaroo skewers and fluorescent cowboy hats. The continued existence of the fair reminds us that such celebrations were not always comfortable; tat was sold in the Middle Ages as well as in the twenty-first century, dealers tricked the innocent and girls 'got into trouble', while children scavenged the fields around the fair in the early morning for money that had been dropped out of trouser pockets. The Irish Tourist Board promoted the Fair in the 1960s and early 1970s, but by the late 1970s and 1980s it was downplayed. Even in the 1960s Muriel Rukeyser had to listen to numerous local people trying to dissuade her from going to the fair – all of which, of course, made her more determined than ever to go. A feast of drunken revelry was not the image of Ireland the Irish Tourist Board, or indeed local Kerry people, wanted to promote. Perhaps out of its time, the fair continues. The Gathering Day. The Fair Day. The Scattering Day. The clink of coins, hare and horse and bull, the roar of beasts, dogs barking – all the sounds and smells and sights as old as time.

Harvest Traditions

The Auld Lammas Fair at Ballycastle has always been a more sedate affair and seems more closely linked with the traditions of the Harvest Home, a tradition much stronger in the north of Ireland than in the south, perhaps because of English and Scottish influences and the religious influence of the Protestant religions. The Festival of the Harvest Thanksgiving is still an important part of the religious year in the Protestant tradition all over Ireland, a joyful, family feast with the churches filled with the fruits of the harvest and religious services held.

The National Folklore Collection's lack of material from Northern Ireland results in a paucity of records on these harvest traditions. The folklorist Kevin Danaher notes that the parts of the country where harvest knots were made and worn by young men and women as love tokens tended to be those heavily settled by the Normans and the English. We do know that the Cailleach, or Granny, the last sheaf, was often kept in the eaves of the house from the end of one harvest to another, or sometimes used to make crosses on St Brighid's Day. There was the tradition of 'putting out the hare from the last sheaf', chasing the animal from its last resort in the cornfield. The hare itself is linked with the Hag and with witches. Girls traditionally tied the sheaves, but in some areas it was the task of an old woman to bind the last sheaf, the work of the Granny, the Cailleach. The Granny was also the name given to the last potato dug, in a harvest that continued through September and into October. In some parts of the country, a communal meal for the harvesters would be held and music and dancing followed to celebrate the end of the labour. Harvest, and Lughnasa generally, was the most communal of the Irish seasons, in terms of both work and play. Participation in the meitheal, the term used for a group effort to help a neighbour with his harvest (or any other large task), was at its height at this time of year.

Summer's End

By now, green growth has choked pathways with brambles, covered hillsides with ferns grown to human height; growth has been as wild as a wild night at Puck Fair. And then the green sea of leaves and light becomes shadowy and the shadows turn darker, a green that begins to feel slightly claustrophobic. What was light and filled with light, now becomes dense and heavy, overspills into decay. As time moves on and the light lessens, the outline of bushes and ferns will start to become ragged and growth will begin to shrink into itself. The green world becomes frayed around the edges, letting the light through in dappled patterns that alter with every gust of wind. The year has unfurled to the zenith of its growth and now it is time for it to enfold. The angle of the sun's light changes, for now it has a new relationship with the earth. The slanting brightness dances, glances off the green of leaves and purple blackberries. Swallows gather. Later, the starlings will flock and swoop in murmurations, Dervish dances that leave the watcher dizzy and awed. Starlings love to perform above wide open fields. In January 2019, a huge flock was spotted, at Screggan near Birr – flying in breathtaking patterns just over the fields where the Ploughing Championships had been held the previous year.

THE WOLFHOUND'S STORY: THE BIRTH OF BRAN

Setanta becomes a dog in name, but there is also a legend where a princess is actually turned into one. Fionn's aunt, Tuireann, was transformed by magic into a wolfhound. In this form she became the mother of the legendary hounds, Bran and Scéolan. Bran was Fionn's most beloved hound. He is described thus: 'a ferocious, small-headed, white-breasted, sleek-haunched hound, having the eyes of a dragon, the claws of a wolf, the vigour of a lion, the venom of a serpent angered to speedy action, (led by) by a massy chain of old silver attached to a collar of brightly-burnished gold around his neck.' But Bran was also the gentlest of hounds, who dipped his tail in milk to lure home a calf when it went missing. I love the story of his birth, this story of girl into hound into girl … but I do sometimes wonder if Tuireann, a princess once again, felt sad at the loss of her wild life, her life as a hound, hunting on the hills.

~

The first thing you should know about me is that I am a princess.

The second thing is that I was once a dog.

Let's make this as clear as possible, I was a princess before I was a dog. And then …

But perhaps I should start at the beginning.

***

Sixteen years old and pretty, though I say so myself, I fell in love with a young prince called Iollan. Dark-haired and dark-eyed, a skilled warrior with a smile that would break your heart. I could tell that he quite liked me too. There was, however, a problem, and when the witch Uchtdealbh — some of the stories call her a Fairy Woman but let's call a spade a spade and a witch a witch — saw us one day up on the hills together, she wasn't happy at all. Because she liked Iollan too.

I have a feeling that Iollan gave her more encouragement than he ever told me, but whatever, I was the one he chose to ask Fionn for in marriage, and I went with him to his palace in the north and was happy and beloved and very soon pregnant.

Uchtdealbh followed us. She came to me one day when I was alone in the Grianán and took her hazel wand out from under her cloak and waved it at me, and there I was, no longer a pretty princess but a fine white wolfhound. At least she left me blonde. I was about to take off back to Almu and the protection of Fionn, when she grabbed me by the neck, slipped a collar over my head and dragged me to the house of a man called Fergus. Fergus had a bad reputation. He was a nasty, unsociable piece of work to humans but a terror to dogs. Indeed, he was famous for hating every kind of dog, whether they were big or small, hairy or smooth, male or female, whether they were slobberers and leg gropers or ladies like me.

'You will have to look after this dog,' said Uchtdealbh to Fergus.

'I will not,' growled Fergus. 'What would I be doing with a dog? I hate them. You must be demented to even ask such a thing of me.'

'Fionn has commanded it,' said Uchtdealbh. 'He has said

you must take her out hunting every day, wear her out with work, and not feed her very much. You can be as mean to her as you like; she needs to be disciplined.'

I tried to make the idiot see that the witch was lying through her teeth but humans are dense sometimes. After much grumbling, the man dragged me to a barn and tied me up. I howled.

I howled for my palace and my friends, for my fine clothes and the admiring looks of men, I howled for my brother and my throne and the food and drink of the feasts of Almu.

I knew I was taking a risk with my howling. It could have gone either way. Fergus could have taken me and beaten me. But I had sensed something when I saw the man. I had seen how lonely he was. And I had seen something else; I had smelled fear and noticed how his hand shook a little when he took my collar. The witch had made a mistake. It wasn't that Fergus hated dogs, it was that he was afraid of them.

I howled so loud and so long that eventually, Fergus came out to the barn and stood at the door and roared at me.

'Will you shut up, you bitch?'

I whined and wagged my tail and put my head to one side and gave him an entreating look. It had worked for me before and it worked for me now. With very bad grace and a lot of curses, Fergus dragged me back into the house and told me I could sleep at the fire. I kept howling.

'What is it now, creature?' said Fergus.

I stared at his bed. He threw his eyes up to heaven.

'Just for tonight then. Until you get settled in.'

I slept well that night. I woke him up by licking his face. We looked into each other's eyes and Fergus saw that I would never hurt him. And I saw that he would never hurt me.

Life was ... different. Nobody listened to me when I looked for food. I was fed when Fergus decided and that was that. At first I was confused by the fact that everything was now seen from a lower level, and a lot happened out of my eyeline, unless I remembered to look up. Not having fingers was a definite disadvantage. But the way I could hear and smell more than made up for this. The smelling especially. When I led Fergus on the hunt, I always found our prey. Oh, those days on the hills, the last warmth of summer changing into the first chill of winter ... the smells that came in on those winds! All life was in those smells, hare and fox and badger, the smell of crops growing and the honey of bees, the smell of wet fern and new black-berries, of hogs roasting twenty miles away and a woman churning milk over the next hill. I followed my nose to the places where an eagle had killed a young hare and left it to ripen on a rock on a hillside, to where a stag was feeding in the heart of the forest, to where a flock of wild ducks had landed on a bogland lake. I became a great huntress, and in the end Fergus grew so fond of dogs that he started up a famous pack, and I became the leader, the princess of the pack. I cast my eye on a young dog from the west and we managed to have a good time for ourselves, on a day we both 'got lost' up on the mountain.

The puppies inside me grew and I gave birth to a boy and a girl hound, Bran and Scéolan.

And soon after, three men and a woman arrived at Fergus's house. Fionn had heard that I had disappeared from Iollan's palace, and he had gone to him with the champion Lugaidh and challenged him on the pain of death to find me. Iollan brought them to Uchtdealbh, who promised to find me if Iollan would take her as his wife. I like to think Iollan had no choice but to cast me away; but let's be honest, he had not exactly been rushing off to find me himself.

And now here they all were, Uchtdealbh and Iollan and Lugaidh and Fionn. I ran to my nephew and licked his face. He looked in my eyes and did not know me, but he did not push me away. Fionn was a friend to dogs. I went to Iollan and he pushed me away. 'Get away, you big hairy mutt,' he said. But Lugaidh took my head between his hands and looked into my eyes and kissed me on the crown of my head.

Fergus greeted Fionn and said, 'I hope you are not coming to take the Hound back, for she is the best of hounds and I have lost my heart to her. I hope you do not mind me calling her Hound for that is the name that the woman who brought her called her; she never told me any other.'

'What woman?' Fionn asked sharply.

'The lady Uchtdealbh,' said Fergus, bowing in her direction.

'That bitch,' said Fionn. 'I would never ask her to do anything for me. And from what I have heard about you, you would be the last person I would ask to look after a dog. I thought you hated them.'

'Hey there,' I said. 'Enough with the bitch word. Witch, say it. Witch.' Everyone ignored me.

Fergus said: 'I used not to like dogs, but Hound is different. She has taught me how wonderful dogs are. But I don't understand. Are you sure you didn't ask me to look after your dog?'

Now Lugaidh said: 'I think you will find that this white hound is more closely related to you than you think, Fionn. What have you to say, Uchtdealbh?'

'Oh, very well,' said the witch sulkily. 'I will change her back.'

She took her hazel wand; and it was the work of a moment for me to be a girl again, though my hair had grown so long that it reached to my knees. Fergus went bright red and rushed to cover me with his cloak and I smiled at him, but he would not look me in the eyes.

I went back to Almu. Iollan went with Uchtdealbh. He gazed at me with his calf's eyes as he left, begging forgiveness. I doubted if he would ever have come to look for me if my nephew had not threatened to part his head from his body. So what I really wanted to do was give him a quick nip, but ladies can't.

Back home, all my friends welcomed me and I had all the things that I thought I had missed so much. But now I missed the things I had learned to love. I took comfort in my puppies, who had come with us as Fionn's hunting dogs. I married Lugaidh, who told me that he had loved me forever. I married him because he alone had seen me for myself when I was in the form of a hound and because he is a kind and faithful man. I had a child with him, who I loved very much. I was happy, mostly.

But a day came when I could bear it no longer and I made

my escape from palace and husband and child and ran into the mountains. As the sun set, I sat on the side of an upland moor and howled. All the small birds of the moor ran away crying, and a hare, disturbed by the noise, bounded across the line of my vision. Oh, how I wanted to chase it. But there was no chance of catching it now.

All I could do was howl.

At first I thought I was howling for Iollan.

Then I realised it was not his loss that was troubling me.

Then I thought I howled for the loss of my innocence and belief in the goodness of men. But then I realised that it was not that I was howling for.

What I was howling for was the world that was closed to me now. I sat on the hillside and howled and howled for my life as a dog. For the scents that were lost to me forever, the smells of the badger's lair and the wet woods. For the feel of rock and grass and ferns under my paws, and the wind on my coat on a stormy winter's day, running wild in the hills after the hare, the fox, the deer. For the long days of the hunt, for the sound of the horn and my companions calling me to come along with them, far ahead of the stumbling, slow-footed humans. For my keen ears, for my wonderful speed in the chase, for my freedom. I howled for a long, long time. Never let it be said that dogs are more faithful than girls.

Hunting Season

I have heard a red beagle's cry on the slope beside the stream
… although my heart is sore, nevertheless the cry is musical
to me.

Duanaire Finn

By the equinox on 22 September, the fields have been shorn
of crops, the main crop potatoes are being harvested, and the
sun's heat has greatly lessened. Stubble remains. The nights
are longer and the shadows come earlier, with that peculiarly
beautiful slant of sun that is seen around the autumn equinox and the winter solstice. September is a month of clearing, cleaning, digging. In September, there was another, now
almost forgotten festival. Michaelmas, St Michael's feast, is
now only really remembered as a legal or academic term, or a
type of ornamental daisy.

Michael is the warrior archangel, who like Lugh kills one
of his own tribe, in this case Satan, who is also Lucifer, the
proud angel, the creature of brightness that fell into darkness.
Michael is associated with high places and most strikingly
with the Skellig Michael island monastery, a handful of stone
huts dating from the sixth century, perched on jagged rocks
far out to sea off the southwest coast of Ireland. This was a
sacred site before Christianity came to Ireland, with stories
connecting the islands to the Tuatha Dé Danaan and with
megalithic remains as well as Christian ones. The Skelligs are
the most westerly point of the pilgrimage routes that criss-
crossed Europe as far as the Levant in the Middle Ages.

September, Michael's month, is the traditional time to make the journey to the Skelligs, though during Lent was another traditional visiting time, as it was possible to get married on the islands when you could not do so on the mainland. But while St Michael was a popular saint, or rather archangel, in Ireland, there is little folk activity associated with Michaelmas, though fowls were killed and eaten. However, if we look back beyond the Celts we once again see strong connections with megalithic structures. Knowth and Dowth and a number of other passage tombs are closely aligned with the movements of the sun at the autumn equinox.

The mists begin, the mushrooms spring up overnight in the pastures and the woods, the world around us changes once again. The haze of September has become the heavy, dank mist of October, beautiful in a different way from the mellowness of early autumn. St Michael's Day traditionally marked the beginning of the hunting season. And the hunt begins. Permissions to kill follow, one after the other. Grouse can legally be shot from mid-August, 'the glorious twelfth', and then the list of prey goes on – from partridge to pheasant, to duck and woodcock. Mountain hares can be shot from August, deer from the first of September. The killing season continues until March.

At the time of the Fianna, hunting was a necessary activity; the meat was needed for food. It was also seen as an important part of the Fenian identity. The stories of the Fianna emphasise the close companionship between the hunters, with the hounds and also the excitement of the race into the unknown, following an elusive target, journeys that often brought the hunters into the Otherworld. Hunting must also have connected the groups of real, historical hunters at a very deep level. Hunting can still wake some primitive, visceral response even in those who hate the idea of wild things being terrorised and killed for sport. On a cold and foggy October morning, I was in Brittany, on a quiet country road with open fields all around. I had already noticed the cluster of white vans and the man in the orange vest standing with his gun in a field not far away from me. I made my usual plea to the universe that the animal, whatever it was, would escape. Then a stag suddenly broke cover from the small wood beyond the fields, and raced towards the road, sometimes doubling back and twisting around, and finally passing within a few feet of me. The whole experience had lasted no more than one or two minutes. I stood and waited, listening to the wild belling of the hounds and the sound of the horn in the distance, hoping that the dogs would not appear out of the cover of the wood any time soon. And it did seem a long time before they appeared, the stream of deerhounds, red tongues lolling, heavy-browed, huge, the pack a single being intent on the chase. With my own little non-hunting beagle held to heel well out of their path I watched something ancient pass before my eyes and was, in spite of myself, moved. The hounds were followed by five men with rifles, all in fluorescent jackets, all red-faced and slightly overweight, all struggling to keep up, and the illusion of something out of time vanished. I think the stag escaped: the dogs were racing in the opposite direction from where I last saw him heading.

Hunting is not something people talk about much in

Ireland, but there are approximately fifty foxhound packs in the country, twenty-six beagle packs, seventy harriers and three hundred hunt clubs. Traditionally associated with the Anglo-Irish aristocracy of the Big House, apart from getting a gun out to shoot a few rabbits or a fox that has been at the poultry, hunting was not a significant aspect of Irish rural life, even back in the 1930s. But to our ancestors, the hunt was a rite of passage and in many cases a way to access the Otherworld. There are many tales of kings and warriors following a magical deer or flocks of magic birds. The hunt leads the hunter into a relationship with nature that is very specific, albeit one that can hardly be justified in the twenty-first century. It also leads us back into the forest, where we go to meet a man who was not a hunter, but a quarry.

THE FOREST'S STORY: SUIBHNE

Our desire when the wild ducks come
at Samhuin, up to May-day,
in each brown wood without scarcity
to be in ivy-branches.

From *Buile Suibhne*, James G O'Keefe

This hunted one, hiding in the brown wood is the mad king Sweeney, or Suibhne Geilt. He was the king who cursed the cleric Ronan and was cursed in his turn to wander all over Ireland, leaping from tree to tree. Suibhne also threw Ronan's psalter in a lake, but an otter retrieved it, so the saint's anger seems a little disproportionate. (Otters, closely associated with a number of saints, were not always so well-behaved. One of them made the youngest daughter of King Cormac pregnant and she gave birth to a son, Conn). But disproportionate or not, Ronan rang his bell and called a curse onto the king, sending him to roam the forests as a madman.

Sweeney lived the life of the wild things. Hairy and naked and feathered, staglike in his leapings and birdlike in his flight, he was the sovereign of the wilderness. In that wilderness he found his connection with all living things, and discovered poetry.

Stripped bare, scourged by the wind, he tells of the wonder of the trees, the oaks, the alders, blackthorns, apples, yew, ivy, holly; all of them comfort him. He praises the animals, the badgers and deer, the fox cubs. The songs of the birds are the sweetest music to his ears. He forages, hidden and protected by the trees like the holy ones in their cells, nested in the ivy of the wood. He runs with the wolf pack and the red stags.

Mad Suibhne leads us from autumn to winter, bringing us with him towards the belling of the stag, the frost and fire and cold clarity of winter. We learn to endure. In the winter, few people travel through the forest and you may not see another human face from one end of the month to the next. Suibhne shows us how to live with this, and sometimes die with this so that in the spring a passing traveller may find your bones covered with moss and leaves and the first green tendrils of nettle or briar. When I came to write the story of Suibhne's madness, I found that I could not make a narrative of it, for Suibhne is the storyteller that will not come inside, the wild part of us that tells no narrative but that of the leaves rustling, or water flowing.

~

Be quiet now.

Look up and listen. My voice is very slow, for my tale is told in the buds, the leaves and the branches, the fruit, the flowers. The twigs and the nuts, the berries, the beech-mast, the acorns, the hazels. So many hazels. The rings that form, each telling the story of the year.

Look down. There is the tale told through the life of my floor. Fallen leaves, all the various shapes of the oak and the hazel, the thorn tree, the alder, the birch and the rowan.

Still upright, shining green and red through the winter, the sharp-tongued holly. The mushrooms and fungi, brown and orange and gold, dun and faintly green, bright red, dotted with white spots. Small white bones crunch underfoot, or is that the sound of dead leaves crackling? Look deeper in. Let me pull you into the soft bed of loam and decay, such very fertile decay. Further down, we are all one in the darkness. But let me not frighten you.

We are back with our feet on the ground. A leaf falls and then flies upwards; you realise that it was no leaf, but a small bird flying. A skaldcrow calls.

***

How Suibhne loved the branchy thorny wilderness, the paradise of light through leaves, droplets falling and the light shining through them. The wind comes up, and the leaves whirl down like a golden snowstorm, each single leaf making its own path, some whirling like dervishes, some dropping gently, carried on the breeze like a hawk circling.

Listen to the baying and the belling, the melodious chant of the hounds, far more beautiful that any cleric's bell or prayer.

There was May Day in the forest, with apple blossom and blackthorn and all the birds singing; there was the silence of winter when cold bit deep into his bones and the wind howled fiercely and there was no food but what could be scavenged from the scavengers, or a handful of watercress on the banks of a stream. There was the smell of the wood at different times of the year, and the music it played.

The stag belled in autumn; the wolf howled in winter and in the spring there was the call of the cuckoo and black-bird. In summer the bees and flies hummed and buzzed. There was the smooth trunk of the birch and the rough-ness of hawthorn, the greeting of thorns and the farewell of soft catkins. The cold of snow, the crack of ice on a stream and the soft cool glide of water over aching feet on a summer's day.

Suibhne would tell you his story, but he has forgotten how to speak. Like an animal, he goes down on all fours and laps milk from the hollow of dried dung.

Once he was a king with a loving wife, Eorann. He was cursed by St Ronan, for he became angry at the sound of the cleric's bell. He disrespected the saint and laid rough hands on him and threw his psalter in a lake. And Ronan cursed him so that at the battle of Moira, Suibhne threw off his clothes and went leaping through the trees, as if the very devil was after him. And from that day on shunned the company of men and women.

Let me tell more.

How he lived for years in the forest, leaping from tree to tree, journeying all over Ireland, and grew hairy and feath-ered at the same time.

How he was tricked by a friend who wanted to turn him into a man again, and was made peaceful for a while. But when his friend Loingseacháin went out to harvest, the Hag of the Mill mocked Suibhne and in retaliation he showed her how he could leap; and he leapt away from humankind once again.

How he refused the comfort of his wife Eorann, telling her that he preferred the company of the birds and the beasts of the wood to that of any female. Yet when she found another man, he wept at her window.

How he found a companion, another Wild Man of the Woods, but they did not keep each other company for long.

How he found comfort at last in a quiet river valley, where the trees edge the water and where the gentle St Moling lived, but he was killed by a jealous husband, a herdsman who thought he was sleeping with his wife, with no cause.

How in the end, the king cursed by a saint was blessed by a saint and was laid in the earth near the banks of the Barrow river. And Moling sang over him, as the beasts and birds gathered and watched, a peaceable assembly. And then they covered him in clay and leaves and left him to rest, held by, sleeping in, the brown wood.

The End of the Year

Each of us is alone on the heart of the earth
pierced by a ray of sun:
and suddenly it's evening.

Salvatore Quasimodo

The weather changes. The last swallows have left. Did you know that if you rob a swallow's nest the cows will milk blood? The days grow short and cold and the leaves turn to dull brown and then are blown away in one of the many storms that rage over the country. There are still golden days, but the knowledge of change is coming. The Fianna put away their weapons of battle.

The end of October blazes, a last blast of brightness before it is time for the earth to sleep. We burn in the fire of the year's turning. Is it the knowledge of fading and decay that the earth itself feels, and so decides to put on its brightest jewels and go out dancing? There is extravagance in the gesture but no desperation. The dance is a simple showing forth of beauty. There is also a great sense of plenitude, for however much we see, we know that there are still countless treasures hidden. The red and the gold apples hide behind dark green leaves, the blackberries and elderberries glow with a secret purple, lost to our sight behind branches and sheltered by tall grass. The land folds into itself and at the same time opens out for harvest, the bounty that is everywhere, on every bush and on every branch, in every field.

Her cloak is opened wide and she walks through the starry nights, ready to wrap us up for winter.

AFTERWORD

Only connect.

EM Forster

The year 2020 was when *The Turning of the Year* was written, the year when we all shared a common threat, were all connected by fear and grief, while at the same time feeling the loss of human connection, of contact with our communities and with loved ones. What I have tried to do in this book is to create the experience of connectedness that I spoke about in the introduction, to interweave story and traditional ways, to give some sense of the closely woven web of nature, heritage and the human community. I have also tried to explore the possibility that while we may be looking at nature, it may be looking back at us. If a saint can turn to a deer, a goddess a crow, a princess a river, have we not all within us the possibility of being part of each other? Indeed, are we not, by our very presence together in this time and place, already just that?

This connectedness comes with responsibilities, with the need for a fundamental change in our attitude to the earth. We have seen how nature's resources are not infinite, but have been and are being consumed and destroyed by our greed. In Ireland, we have seen the forests cut, the potato crop fail, the bogs stripped. And with each act of destruction, our planet, our country and we ourselves have lost something, have been made less. The problem is not just an Irish but an international one. Most of the world has already jumped onto the bandwagon of industrial farming. The amount of cultivation being done on an industrial scale, from tree growing to chicken farming, has caused enormous problems in terms of the environment, problems so huge that we can often feel helpless in the face of them.

Internationally, much of the industrialisation of the farming landscape is rooted in our human need to survive. The very cheap food that is making us fat and unhealthy is produced by people who are getting very little recompense and so need to produce more and more in order to keep themselves and their families alive. Intensive dairy farming increases carbon emissions and drastically decreases biodiversity. Arable farming is currently dependent on a high use of pesticides and in its usual form is also lethal to biodiversity, especially with the wide-scale destruction of ditches, banks and hedgerows that is such a feature of its practice. The fieldmice, the hares, the hawks and the foxes cannot survive such destruction. It's as if we humans have decided that any creature or plant that cannot be bought or sold has no home in our landscape.

> When we are driving the cows home we say hi home hi home. When we are calling the calves home we say suck, suck, suck. When we are calling the pigs we say bock, bock, bock. When we are calling the hens we say chuck, chuck, chuck.
>
> National Folklore Collection

It would be very naive to think that all animals were treated well at all times by our ancestors, but there was certainly a closer relationship, a deeper connection between beast and human than is possible now in industrial-sized farms. There was also a closer relationship between the farmer and the land, the trees that grow on it, the rocks that rise out of it, the wind that blows across it, the rain that falls and the sun that shines on it. There was a tacit admission that nature could not be controlled by human will, but by developing a relationship of respect with it. This same respect was shown by fishermen in the traditions associated with the sea. The kingdom of the sea itself contains worlds of lore and legend, which cannot be explored here.

The Sídh or fairies were to some extent the embodiment of nature; they could be malicious, wilful, and never predictable, and they had to be supplicated. Give them milk on May Day rather than have your cows go dry for the year; and if the fairy should take the form of a saint, be sure that saint is respected and treated well also. I am not advocating a belief in either saints or Sídh. I have no answers, but only an intuition that Mother Nature, embodied in her animals, her pastures, her woods, has nurtured us for millennia and needs us to nurture her too. It is time for humanity to grow up.

The need to find a way to rebalance our relationship with nature has become ever more urgent. Our time is running out. If we cannot grow food we cannot live. As has been said many times before, we are burning our house down with us inside it. The seasons, which enabled the beginning of farming – the surety that there will be sun and rain for the crops to grow and that the pasture the cows grazed on will not become a mudslide in winter or a dustbowl in summer – are themselves under threat because of climate change, change that is a direct result of human activity. We will never be able to change our actions if we do not also create change within ourselves. We need to change, to move, not necessarily forward, but into a different way of being.

THE MUSIC OF WHAT HAPPENS

We have seen how ritual is a way for the individual and the community to accept change, to navigate the passage from one state of being to another – from winter to summer, from night to day, from life to death. Ritual enabled and encouraged humans to enter into an acknowledgement of all that is 'other', while at the same time acknowledging that the other is part of ourselves. At its deepest levels, ritual can transmute, take on a new form and affirm something beyond us as individuals. The theologian Thomas Berry describes the universe as a liturgy, a constant celebratory ritual, and he sees the human being as the creature in which the universe celebrates itself. Through marking the cycles – the cycles of our individual bodies, of night and day, of the seasons – we acknowledge that we are part of something that goes beyond 'me and mine'. No matter whether the ritual is individual or communal, by participating in it we acknowledge our connectedness to our communities, beyond our communities to humankind, and beyond even our species to that vastness that is too big for any single human mind to grasp. We are told that the Anthropocene era is upon us, and in the 1970s, in his book *The Stations of the Sun*, Ronald Hutton was claiming that 'Humanity has come to replace the natural world at the centre of the wheel of the year.' Perhaps it is time to rethink that placement. For in refusing to connect to the otherness that we are part of, we are condemning ourselves to loneliness, as individuals and as a species. If we revisit the old rituals and rid them of the dogma we have associated with them, we may be able to create new ways in which we can engage with the spirit of communal awe that they invoke. The joy of this approach is that it needs no laws, no teachers, no leaders; no one to set up rules and limits, to tell us what we can or we can't do. It is an approach very much in the spirit of Suibhne and Boann, of Caoilte listening for the wolf's call, of Brighid sheltering the fox and Kevin holding his palm open for the blackbird's egg. In this approach to the world and to time, the year doesn't end; it becomes new and we are made new with the year, along with everything that grows, with everything that dies.

We watch the darkness fall. There in the deep and wonderful darkness we find a deep and wonderful silence. Then, again, the music begins. Always, the music begins.

BIBLIOGRAPHY

Books

Attenborough, David, *A Life on Our Planet*, Ebury Press, London, 2020.

Bell, Margaret, *The Old Lammas Fair of Ballycastle*, Moyle District Council, Ballycastle, 1966.

Berry, Thomas, *The Dream of the Earth*, Counterpoint, Berkeley, 1988.

Carmichael, Alexander, *Carmina Gadelica*, Vols 1 and 11, Edinburgh, 1900.

Carney, James, *Medieval Irish Lyrics*, The Dolmen Press, Dublin, 1967.

Clarke, Austin, *Collected Poems,* Carcanet Press Ltd, Manchester, 2008.

Colum, Padraic, (ed.) *A Treasury of Irish Folklore*, Wings Books, New York, 1992.

Connolly, Linda, *The Irish Family*, Routledge, London, 2014.

Cooney, Gabriel, *Landscapes of Neolithic Ireland*, Routledge, London, 1999.

Cooney, Gabriel, 'Sacred and Secular Neolithic Landscape in Ireland' in *Sacred Sites, Sacred Places*, edited by David L. Carmichael et al., Routledge, 1994, Oxford.

Costello, Eugene, *Transhumance and the Making of Ireland's Uplands, 1550–1900*, Boydell & Brewer, Boydell Press, UK and USA, 2020.

Cross, Eric, *The Tailor and Ansty*, Mercier Press, Cork and Dublin, 1943.

Cross, Tom Peete, and Clarke, Harris Slover, *Ancient Irish Tales*, Barnes and Noble, New York, 1996.

Danaher, Kevin, *Irish Customs and Beliefs, Gentle Places, Simple Things*, Mercier Press, Cork, 2012.

Danaher, Kevin, *The Year in Ireland*, Mercier Press, Cork, 1972.

Davidson, HR Ellis, *Myths and Symbols in Pagan Europe*, Syracuse University Press, New York, 1988.

Deeney, David, *Peasant Lore from Gaelic Ireland*, D Nutt, London, 1900.

Dillon, Myles, *Irish Sagas*, Stationery Office, Dublin, 1959.

Dooley, Ann and Roe, Harry, (translators), *Tales of the Elders of Ireland*, Oxford University Press, Oxford, 1999.

Douglas, Mary, *Purity and Danger*, Routledge & Kegan Paul, London, 1966.

Eogan, George, *Knowth and the Passage Tombs of Ireland*, Thames and Hudson, New York, 1986.

Estyn Evans, E, *Irish Folk Ways*, Routledge & Kegan Paul, London, 1972.

Frazer, James, *The Golden Bough*, Oxford University Press, Oxford, 2009.

Glob, PV, *The Bog People*, Paladin, London 1972.

Gose, Elliott B, Jr., *The Irish Wonder Tale, An Introduction to the Study of Fairy Tales*, Brandon, Dingle, 1985.

Green, Miranda, *The Gods of the Celts*, The History Press, Stroud, 2011.

Gregory, Augusta, *Lady Gregory's Complete Irish Mythology*, Smithmark, London, 2000.

Gwynn, Edward, *The Metrical Dindshenchas*, Royal Irish Academy, Dublin, 1905.

Hall, Samuel and Anna, *Hall's Ireland: Mr. & Mrs.Hall's Tour of 1840*, Sphere, London, 1984.

Harbison, Peter, *Pre-Christian Ireland, from the First Settlers to the Early Celts*, Thames and Hudson, London, 1988.

Hardy, Philip Dixon, *Legends, Tales and Stories of Ireland*, Forgotten Books, London, 2018.

Heaney, Seamus, *New Selected Poems 1966–1987*, Faber and Faber, London, 1990.

Heaney, Seamus, *Sweeney Astray*, Faber and Faber, London, 1994.

Hull, Eleanor, *Pagan Ireland*, Palala Press, 2015.

Hull, Eleanor, *The Gods of the Gael*, AlbaCraft Kindle Edition, Inverness, 2018.

Hyde, Douglas, *Legends of Saints and Sinners*, Wentworth Press, 2019.

Jackson, Kenneth, *Studies in Early Celtic Nature Poetry*, Cambridge University Press, Cambridge, 2011.

Joyce, PW, *Old Celtic Romances*, The Talbot Press, Dublin, 1962.

Joyce, PW, *Old Irish Folk Music and Songs*, Hodges, Figgis, & Co., Ltd, Dublin, 1909.

Joyce, PW, *The Wonders of Ireland,* Longmans, Green, and Co., London, New York, 1911.

Kavanagh, Patrick, *Collected Poems*, Allen Lane, London, 2004.

Kerrigan, Jo, *Follow the Old Road, Discover the Ireland of Yesteryear*, The O'Brien Press, Dublin, 2015.

Knowlson, T Sharper, *The Origins of Popular Superstitions*, Senate, Twickenham, 1998.

Lebor Gabála Eireann, translated and edited by RA Stewart MacAlister, 1938.

Logan, Patrick, *The Old Gods, The Facts About Irish Fairies*, Appletree Press, Belfast, 1981.

Lucas, AT, *The Sacred Trees of Ireland*, Cork Historical and Archaeological Society, Cork, 1963.

Lucas, AT, *Cattle in Ancient Ireland*, Boethius Press Ltd, UK, 1989.

Lysaght, Patricia, *The Banshee, The Irish Death Messenger*, Roberts Rinehart, USA, 1997.

Mac Coitir, Niall, *Ireland's Animals, Myths, Legends and Folklore*, Collins Press, Cork, 2015.

Mac Coitir, Niall, *Ireland's Birds, Myths, Legends and Folklore*, Collins Press, Cork, 2015.

Mac Coitir, Niall, *Ireland's Wild Plants, Myths, Legends and Folklore*, Collins Press, Cork, 2015.

Mac Coitir, Niall, *Irish Trees, Myths, Legends and Folklore*, Collins Press, Cork, 2003.

Mac Neill, Máire, *The Festival of Lughnasa*, Oxford University Press, Oxford, 1962.

Magan, Manchán, *Thirty-Two Words for Field*, Gill Books, Dublin, 2020.

Mallory, JP, *In Search of Irish Dreamtime*, Thames and Hudson Ltd, London, 2016.

McDonald, Bridget Theresa, *Booleying in Achill: Booleying in Achill, Achillbeg and Corraun: survey, excavation and analysis of booley settlements in the Civil Parish of Achil*, Thesis, NUI Galway, 2014.

McKone, Kim, *Pagan Past and Christian Present in Early Irish Literature*, An Sagart, Maynooth, 1990.

McMann, Jean, *Loughcrew and the Cairns*, After Hours Books, Oldcastle, 1993.

Meyer, Kuno, *Hail Brigit: An Old Irish Poem on the Hill of Alenn*, Leopold Classic Library, 2017.

Meyer, Kuno, *Selections from Ancient Irish Poetry*, Leopold Classic Library, 2015.

Murphy, Anthony and Moore, Richard, *Island of the Setting Sun*, Liffey Press, Dublin, 2020.

Murphy, Gerard, (ed. and translator), *Duanaire Finn*, Irish Texts Society, Dublin, 1935.

Murray, Patrick, *The Deer's Cry, A Treasury of Irish Religious Verse*, Four Courts Press, Dublin, 1986.

Ní Ghríofa, Doireann, *A Ghost in the Throat*, Tramp Press, Dublin, 2020.

Ó Catháin, Seamus, *Irish Life and Lore*, Mercier Press, Cork, 1982.

Ó Corráin, Donnchada, Breatnach, Liam and McCone, Kim, (eds.), *Sages, saints and storytellers: Celtic Studies in honour of Professor James Carney*, An Sagart, Maynooth, 1989.

Ó Crualaoich, Gearóid, *The Book of the Cailleach*, Cork University Press, Cork, 2006.

Ó Duinn, Seán, *Where Three Streams Meet*, Columba Press, Dublin, 2000.

Ó Duinn, Seán, *The Rites of Brigid*, Columba Press, Dublin, 2005.

Ó hÓgáin, Dáithí, *The Lore of Ireland, An Encyclopaedia of Myth, Legend and Romance*, Collins Press, Cork, 2006.

Ó hÓgáin, Dáithí, *The Sacred Isle: Belief and Religion in pre-Celtic Ireland*, Collins Press, Cork, 1999.

O'Keeffe, JG, translator and editor, *Buile Suibhne (The Frenzy Of Suibhne) Being The Adventures Of Subhne Geilt, A Middle Irish Romance*, Irish Texts Society, London, 1913.

O'Hanlon, John, *Legend Lays of Ireland*, Palala Press, 2015.

O'Kelly, Michael, *Newgrange; Archaeology, Art and Legends*, Thames and Hudson, London, 1982.

Ó Súilleabháin, Sean, *Irish Wake Amusements*, Mercier Press, Cork, 1997.

Ó Súilleabháin, Sean, *Storytelling in Irish Tradition*, Published for the Cultural Relations Committee of Ireland by Mercier Press, Cork, 1973.

Ó Súilleabháin, Sean, *Irish Folk Customs and Belief*, Published for the Cultural Relations Committee of Ireland by Mercier Press, Cork, 1977.

O'Sullivan, Humphrey, *The Diary of Humphrey O'Sullivan, 1780–1837*, Mercier Press, Cork, 1993.

Pedlar, Kit, *The Quest for Gaia*, Souvenir Press, London, 1979.

Pochin Mould, Daphne, *Ireland of the Saints*, Batsford, London, 1953.

Raftery, Barry, *Pagan Celtic Ireland; The Enigma of the Irish Iron Age*, Thames and Hudson, London 1994.

Riordan, Maurice, (ed.) *The Finest Music, an Anthology of Early Irish Lyrics*, Faber, London, 2014.

Rolleston, TW, *Myths and Legends of the Celtic Race*, George C Harrap, London, 1911.

Ross, Anne, *Pagan Celtic Britain*, Cardinal, London, 1974.

Rukeyser, Muriel, *The Orgy*, New English Library, London, 1965.

Saramago, Quasimodo, tr. Jack Bevan, *Complete Poems*, Carcanet Press, Manchester, 2007.

Shepherd, Nan, *The Living Mountain*, Canongate, London, 2011.

Spenser, Edmund, *Collected Works*, Dodo Press, London, 2015.

Stokes, Whitley T and Westropp, W, (eds.) *Tales from the Dindshenchas*, AlbaCraft Publishing, Kindle Edition, Inverness, 2007.

Thomas, Keith, *Religion and the Decline of Magic*, Penguin, London, 1991.

Traherne, Thomas, *Centuries of Meditations*, Cosimo Classics, New York, 2007.

Turner, Vincent, *Dramas, Fields and Metaphors, Symbolic Action in Human Society*, Cornell University Press, Ithaca and London, 1974.

Waddell, John, *Archaeology and Celtic Myth*, Four Courts Press, Dublin, 2015.

Wentz, WY Evans, *The Fairy Faith in Celtic Countries*, Colin Smythe, Buckinghamshire, 1977.

Whelan, Dolores, *Ever Ancient, Ever New*, Columba Press, Dublin, 2006.

Wilde, Lady, *Ancient Legends of Ireland*, Poolbeg, Dublin, 2000.

Wilde, William, *An inquiry into the time of the introduction and the general use of the potato in Ireland, and its various failures since that period. Also, a notice of the substance called bog butter,* MH Gill, Dublin, 1856.

Wilde, William, *The Beauties of the Boyne and its Tributary the Blackwater*, The Sign of the Three Candles, Dublin, 1949.

Yeats, WB, *The Poems*, JM Dent, London, 1990.

Young, Rosamund, *The Secret Life of Cows*, Faber and Faber, London, 2018.

Zuchelli, Christine, *The Sacred Trees of Ireland*, Collins Press, Cork, 2016.

Journals and Articles

Breen, Richard, 'The Ritual Expression of Interhousehold Relationships in Ireland', Cambridge Anthropology, Vol. 6, No. 1/2, (Spring/Summer 1980), pp. 33–59.

Carey, John, 'Time, Memory and the Boyne Necropolis', *Proceedings of the Harvard Celtic Colloquium*, Vol. 10 (1990), pp. 24–36.

Christiansen, Reidar, Th,, 'Some Notes on the Fairies and the Fairy Faith', *Béaloideas*, Iml. 39/41 (1971–1973), pp. 95–111.

Costello, Eugene, 'Temporary freedoms? Ethnoarchaeology of female herders at seasonal sites in northern Europe', *World Archaeology*, (2018), pp. 50:1, pp. 165–184.

Cronin, Mike, 'Projecting the nation through sport and culture, Ireland's Aonach Tailteann and the Irish Free State, 1924– 32', *Journal of Contemporary History*, Vol. 38, No. 3, Sport and Politics (Jul., 2003), pp. 395–411.

Ferguson, Samuel, 'On the Evidences Bearing on Sun-Worship at Mount Callan, Co. Clare', *Proceedings of the Royal Irish Academy. Polite Literature and Antiquities*, Vol. 1 (1879), pp. 265–272, ix.

Hannon, WB, 'Christmas and Its Folk-Lore', *The Irish Monthly*, Vol. 52, No. 607 (Jan. 1924), pp. 20–27.

Hore, Herbert Francis, 'Woods and Fastnesses in Ancient Ireland', *Ulster Journal of Archaeology*, First Series, Vol. 6 (1858), pp. 145–161.

Johnson, Helen Sewell, 'November Eve Beliefs and Customs in Irish Life and Literature', *The Journal of American Folklore*, Vol. 81, No. 320 (Apr.– Jun. 1968).

Lucy, Sean, 'The Poetry of Austin Clarke', *The Canadian Journal of Irish Studies*, Vol. 9, No. 1 (Jun. 1983).

Lysaght, Patricia, *'Visible Death: Attitudes to the dying in Ireland'*, *Merveilles & contes*. Vol. 9, No. 1 (May 1995), pp. 27–60.

MacLeod, Sharon Paice, 'A Confluence of Wisdom: The Symbolism of Wells, Whirlpools, Waterfalls and Rivers in Early Celtic Sources', *Proceedings of the Harvard Celtic Colloquium*, Vol. 26/27 (2006/2007).

Mag Fhloinn, Billy, 'Martinmas Tradition in South-West County Clare: A Case Study'. *Béaloideas*, Iml. 75 (2007), pp. 79–108.

McNeill, John T, Folk, 'Paganism in the Penitentials', *The Journal of Religion*, Vol. 13, Number 4, (Oct. 1933).

Mooney, James, 'The Funeral Customs of Ireland', *Proceedings of the American Philosophical Society*, Vol. 25, No. 128 (Jul.–Dec. 1888), pp. 243–296.

Muller, Sylvie, 'The Irish Wren Tales and Ritual, To Pay or Not to Pay the Debt of Nature', *Béaloideas*, Iml. 64/65 (1996/1997), pp. 131–169.

O' Dowd, Anne, 'Green rushes under your feet! Spreading rushes in folklore and history', *Béaloideas*, Iml. 79 (2011), pp. 82–112.

O'Hare, Patricia, 'St. John's Eve Traditions in County Kerry, c. 1850–1950', *Béaloideas*, Iml. 76 (2008), pp. 23–88.

Ó Madagáin, Breandán, 'Functions of Irish Song in the Nineteenth Century', *Béaloideas*, Iml. 53 (1985), pp. 130–216.

Ó Riain, Pádraig, 'A Study of the Irish Legend of the Wild Man', *Eigse* 14:3 (1972), 179–206.

O'Sullivan, Aidan, 'Exploring past people's interactions with wetland environments in Ireland', *Proceedings of the Royal Irish Academy: Archaeology, Culture, History, Literature*, Vol. 107C (2007), pp. 147–203.

Nagy, JF, 'Liminality and Knowledge in Irish Tradition', *Studia Celtica*, 1981.

Prendergast, John P, 'Of Hawks and Hounds in Ireland', *Transactions of the Kilkenny Archaeological Society*, Vol. 2, No. 1 (1852), pp. 144–155.

CREDITS

PICTURE CREDITS

The author and publisher would like to thank the following for permission to reproduce photographs and illustrative material: Front cover: Shutterstock. Author photograph: City Headshots. Interior of book: pp91, 120, 137, 217 Dublin City Library and Archive; pp26, 28, 35, 64-5, 66, 69 (bottom), 79, 90, 127, 132, 136, 143, 153, 171, 173, 180, 205, 230, 237, 248, 253, 255, 259, 260 Eithne Massey; pp29, 89, 144, 203 Fidelma Massey; pp11, 39, 41, 103, 110, 111, 146, 170, 188 *Illustrated London News* Ltd/Mary Evans Picture Library; pp37, 48, 95, 157, 194-5, 197, 202, 249 Jacques Le Goff; pp61, 80-1, 98, 219 National Folklore Collection, UCD; pp12, 128-9 Shutterstock; p6 Tara Huellou-Meyler; pp53, 164, 211, 224, 235 *Dublin Penny Journal*.

The author and publishers have endeavoured to establish the origin of all in-copyright images and quotations used. If any involuntary infringement of copyright has occurred, sincere apologies are offered, and the owners of such copyright are requested to contact the publisher.

TEXT CREDITS

I would like to thank the Director of the National Folklore Collection, Críostóir Mac Cárthaigh, for permission for the following quotations from the National Schools' Collection: The Schools' Collection, Vol. 0706, p525, Trohanny, Co. Meath. Collector: Patrick Gargan, Teacher: Máire Ní Chreaig; The Schools' Collection, Vol. 1119, p174, Convent of Mercy, Moville, Co. Donegal Informant: Miss Mary O'Donnell, Collector: Kathleen Barr, Teacher Sr. Celestine Clarke; The Schools' Collection, Vol. 0272, p106, Rathpeak, Co. Roscommon. Informant: Kieran Kenny, Collector: Kathleen Kenny, Teacher: Mícheál Mac Ceit; The Schools' Collection, Vol. 0674, p294, Tinure, Co. Louth. Collector: Peggy Mc Cullough, Teacher: S Ó Cathail; 'In older times people went to the public houses and got drunk'; The Schools' Collection, Vol. 0530, p215, Redwood, Co. Tipperary. Teacher: Máighréad Nic Chormaic. Collected from various old people; The Schools' Collection, Vol. 0530, p215, Redwood, Co. Tipperary. Teacher: Máighréad Nic Chormaic. Collected from various old people; The Schools' Collection, Vol. 0713, p273, Slane, Co. Meath. Collector: Ita O'Reilly, Teacher: Josephine Cooney; The Schools' Collection, Vol. 0956, p113, Scotstown, Co. Monaghan. Collector: Maggie Clerkin, Teacher: P Mac Cionnaith; The Schools' Collection, Vol. 0516, p278, Grange,

Co. Limerick. Teacher: Tomás Ó Loínsigh; The Schools' Collection, Vol. 0347, p107, Rathcoola West, Co. Cork. Informant: Mrs O'Brien, Teacher: M Ní Shúilleabháin; The Schools' Collection, Vol. 0866, p105, Muckalee, Kilkenny. Informant: James Walsh, Collector Margaret Walsh, Teacher: P Ó Conchobhair, T Ó Teimhneáin.

The lines from the opening and closing sections of 'The Great Hunger' by Patrick Kavanagh, are reprinted from *Collected Poems* (2004) by kind permission of the Trustees of the Estate of the late Katherine B Kavanagh, through the Jonathan Williams Literary Agency.

The poem *Suddenly it's Evening*, by Salvatore Quasimodo, *tr.* Jack Bevan (*Complete Poems*, 2017) is reprinted by kind permission of Carcanet Press, Manchester, UK.